STORIES FROM THE SPIRITUAL LIFE

VOLUME II

TEJVAN PETTINGER

Copyright © 2021 Tejvan Pettinger

No portion of this book may be reproduced in any form without express written permission from the publisher:

Cover design: Vilas Silverton

ISBN: 978-1-911319-38-2

First Edition went to press: 21 November 2021

PREFACE

These are a few stories inspired by following the spiritual life under the guidance of Sri Chinmoy. Some events are loosely based on real life; sometimes the stories just try to capture the spirit of the spiritual life according to my own understanding and perception.

Sri Chinmoy encouraged his disciples to write as a form of spiritual sadhana and I can attest to the value of his advice. When I do manage to write, I find it can be a very rewarding way to reflect on certain issues and experiences. Writing also helps clarify what improvements we could make in our own spiritual life and - perhaps mostly importantly - encourage us to 'practise what we preach'.

I wrote these stories in 2018 and 2019, shortly after the publication of Stories vol 1. For a few months, I was blessed with the bird of inspiration and wrote at a rapid pace. But, on completion of the writing, the inspiration to publish was sadly lacking and it was quietly put to one side as other tasks become more pressing. As 2022 neared, I made a resolution, it was really time to publish, I could delay no longer!

Re-reading your own writing is not always easy for a writer, as the passage of time can change your perspective and make yourself your own best critic! I was slightly amused to note that in 2019, I had written a story about a spiritual Master encouraging his disciples to get a vaccine. Of course, now I regret my apathy in not publishing sooner, because it might have looked like I had some kind of foresight! I left the story as it was and resisted the temptation to change or edit.

Tejvan Pettinger, Oxford, 21 November 2021.

Your Master

Your Master observes
More than he admits.

Your Master loves
More than he reveals.

Your Master cries
More than you see.

Your Master gives
More than you need.

- Sri Chinmoy [1]

---

1. Sri Chinmoy, *The Wings of Light, part 6*, #272, Aum Press, Puerto Rico, 1974.

STORIES FROM THE SPIRITUAL LIFE, PART 2

ABHIK'S PASSING

"I am sorry to hear of Abhik's passing," said Alex.

"Yes, I will miss him. Though I feel foolish for being sad. He lived such a long time and he was ready to go," said Bahir.

"I know about death and reincarnation from the Master's philosophy. But when it happens, philosophy can only give so much comfort," said Alex.

"Yes. That is true. Recently, I have had quite a lot of practice in attending memorial services of my dear friends – but it can still be hard to say farewell, even if you know it is not permanent. Still there is a sweetness in the sorrow. As the poet Rumi remarked:

> A stone I died and rose again a plant;
> A plant I died and rose an animal;
> I died an animal and was born a man.

Why should I fear? What have I lost by death?

"Yes," said Alex, "poetry about death from our Master and other Seer-Poets really touches something deep in my core. Moving, poignant and elevating all at the same time."

"In Abhik's memorial yesterday, I was struck by the photo of him from his youth. It was just a photo, but at the same time it seemed to be, well, so alive," said Alex.

"Yes, I know what you mean. The Master said that after a person's death, the soul can stay close to earth for a few days. I think Abhik was offering us his final good wishes, before going for a well-earned rest," said Bahir.

"One thing that inspired me about Abhik," said Alex, "was when I learned that for 40 years he had been saying every daily prayer – without fail. The Master gave so many daily prayers I assumed no one would ever manage to do it. I thought just a few would suffice but I saw the joy he got."

"Yes," said Bahir, "Sometimes I think the Master sets such high standards – in the hope we will at least aspire to get part of the way there. But in Abhik's case, he thought: why not just do everything exactly it the way the Master wanted? It was such a simple and beautiful philosophy."

"I will certainly miss Abhik," said Alex, "I spent some considerable time with him in recent years. He seemed removed from the cares of the world. Secure with faith in his Master."

"He was a great seeker," said Bahir, "but he lived through his fair share of challenges. Like us all, he wasn't always floating above the snares of the world! A story that comes to mind. Once the Master said to Abhik that many thousands of years ago, he had been with the Master in a previous incarnation. Back then he had devotedly served the Master. But... and the Master paused and with a hint of a smile said, 'God alone knows what you have been doing for the past 2,000 years!' Now you can make of that what you will. But at other times the Master also hinted how easily it was to get lost in the world. The allure of the world can be too strong even for great souls."

"Yes," said Alex, "it reminds me of the story of Narada –

when he was asked by the great sage Vishnu to get a glass of water. Narada went to earth, but once there he forgot all about his task. He got married, had children and the years flew by."

"That is an illumining story," said Bahir, "I think it is an allegory for human life. We come with a promise to the Supreme, but when we are in the world it is so easy to forget our divine promises. The Master would sometimes mention that the great spiritual Master, Sri Ramakrishna, brought down three liberated souls to serve his Mission: Swami Vivekananda, Swami Brahmananda and a third who never made it – presumably lost in the world."

"Yes," said Alex, "it is mind-blowing that even liberated souls can get lost in worldly life. What hope for us lesser souls?"

"Well, we got lucky," said Bahir. "In the Vedas, it says that even a human incarnation is a great boon that many souls cannot take for granted. But to have a human incarnation and be blessed with a God-realised soul for your Master – this is a one in a billion chance."

"Bahir, would you be keen to come back after you die?" asked Alex.

"Alex, there's still a bit of life in me yet, dear boy!"

"I'm sorry! Here I am 40 years old, and already thinking about future incarnations. I know the Master would say: live for the present. But, at the same time, I would really like to come back to the Master's Path."

"Well," said Bahir, "That is a good aspiration to have. Once the Master was asked, 'How can I make sure I come back to your path in the future?' The Master said the answer was to aspire in this incarnation. If we make the Master's path a constant and living part of ourselves, we will create a powerful thread that will help us come back next time. Also, even if we find ourselves going slower in the spiritual life, we should never give up, because as long as we stay in the boat, we can always pick up our aspiration in a future incarnation – or perhaps even in a few years' time. Sometimes, aspiration deserts us, but equally, if we stay steadfast, we may never know when the Supreme can give us new inspiration."

"I remember one talk the Master gave us many years ago. The essence of the talk was to give everything to this spiritual life. So many incarnations we have had to please ourselves and follow our own way. But, has this brought us happiness or satisfaction? The Master said, 'At least for this incarnation, try and live the spiritual life – wholeheartedly.' We can always go back to our worldly desires in future incarnations. But the Master said that if you do live the spiritual life wholeheartedly for one incarnation, the joy and satisfaction will more than compensate for the so-called sacrifices we think we make."

"It was an interesting insight, because the Master was reminding us to look at the much bigger picture, which we cannot always see. We feel we have such a short time and so many things we want to experience. But the Master sees our whole soul's evolution, from beginning to end."

"Once Sri Ramakrishna was walking with his disciples when they came across a big house, which belonged to a rich man. Now, Sri Ramakrishna wanted to go and visit this rich man, and his disciples were surprised, because usually Sri Ramakrishna had no interest in money or worldly people. But Sri Ramakrishna explained to his disciples, 'In his last incarnation, this rich man was a great seeker who fell from the path of spirituality. However, his years of sadhana had given him much good karma, so he was able to be reborn in a wealthy family.' Ramakrishna now wanted to go and try rekindle this former seeker's latent spiritual hunger."

"Do you think it is a blessing or curse to be born into a wealthy family?" said Alex.

"It very much depends. There is a story about a wise king who had tremendous wealth. Once he went to visit his Guru with many of his poor subjects. As his Guru was meditating there was extreme weather, and so his subjects ran back to their villages to try and protect their possessions. However, the king who had the most to lose sat unmoved at the feet of his Guru. When the Guru finished his meditation, he asked the king why he didn't go back to save his outer wealth like his subjects. The king replied that his real wealth was his inner wealth – why should he give up this inner wealth to try to salvage the meaningless outer wealth? So, in that case, the rich king had greater detachment than those with less wealth. However, outer wealth can be a temptation to a comfortable life. If our outer life is very comfortable, we may feel less inner hunger. But it is not the outer wealth – rather the attachment we have to money – which is the problem. When wealth is used for a divine purpose, it is a veritable boon. But if we are overly attached to wealth, it is a curse for the spiritual life. However, when you remember the transitory nature of life, you realise how fleeting wealth is. As the old saying goes, 'you can't take it with you.'"

DEVOTION

"How was it dealing with the Master on a daily basis?" asked Donald.

"Rakhal tells a funny and illumining story," said Bahir.

"Sometimes when you were dealing with the Master daily, you could forget the Master's spiritual height – absorbed in daily life, disciples could slip into familiar ways of talking. Once the Master was scolding the disciples for being too relaxed or informal in how they would answer the phone to the Master. The Master once rang Bob and Bob replied, 'Can you just hold on a moment?' The Master was intrigued to know what was more important than taking the phone call of your Master. Anyway, the Master had been emphasising the importance of speaking to the Master in a respectful and devoted way. So, a few days later, Rakhal picks up the phone and it is the Master calling. So Rakhal answers as devotedly as he can, making a great effort to be soulful. But the Master retorts, 'Eh Rakhal, why are you talking like a girl!'

"Rakhal felt cut to the quick and spoke in a more normal way. Just to avoid misunderstanding, the Master wasn't being disparaging about the way girls speak – far from it. He was just making Rakhal aware that his attempts to be soulful had unconsciously slipped into trying to be something he wasn't. Real devotion and soulfulness are natural and spontaneous. But sometimes we subconsciously think a particular way of being is how devotion should look, so we try to imitate this mental idea.

"The Master wanted us to be sincere and true to ourselves. For example, the Master said his male disciples should sing in a particular way – deep and strong. His female disciples have a different voice. It is thinner, higher, more ethereal. It is not a matter of comparison or one being better than the other. It is about singing to your respective strengths and natural ability. The problem comes when we think we should try to imitate someone else's sound. But real satisfaction comes from being true to our inherent abilities, talent and nature."

"It is funny how the Master is trying to catch both extremes – being too callous and being too devoted," said Donald.

"Yes," said Bahir, "but I wouldn't say it is about being 'too devoted'. It is very easy for us to place emphasis on the outer forms of devotion – how we speak, how we act, what we offer. But, the Master didn't appreciate the devotion which had a subtle, almost unconscious motivation of looking around to see who is watching us.

"In the Indian tradition, disciples would prostrate themselves at the feet of their Guru. But in our culture, the Master didn't appreciate this kind of display at all. The Master could instantly distinguish between the fake devotion and the real devotion. The real devotion is not in physical offerings or displays, but the inner love and concern for the Master. At the same time, if we are sloppy in our speech, sloppy in how we answer the phone, we are holding back our soul's natural devotion."

"I have read about devotion a lot in the Master's writings, but have never really understood what devotion is," said Donald.

"Me neither," said Bahir. "Maybe it is not something to be understood. It is perhaps more helpful to think of it like a muscle that can get stronger over time – as long as we exercise it. You can't force it. It is better to focus on your spiritual discipline – if you pray, meditate, sing with a one-pointed focus, then you allow the heart's devotion to come to the fore."

"How do you distinguish between the false and true devotion?" asked Donald.

"You have to see whether the ego is involved," said Bahir. "Just feel it is you and the Master, and other people are entirely absent. If it makes no difference, then it is probably real devotion. If we are looking around to see who is noticing our devotion, then our devotion is tinged with an impurity.

"It can be very hard to be aware of our own self-deception. But another thing we can do is spend time with other disciples who are really devoted. Don't imitate, but silently observe. Even after 20 or 30 years on the path, I am always learning from the devotion of other disciples. I'm not even always consciously aware, but for example, did you know the Master even gave instruction for how to pick up one of his books from a bookcase? I'm sure you know for prasad we take with our right or both hands. But, when we take the book, we should do the same – feel we are picking up a sacred object. If we do these little things, it helps to grow our devotion.

There are so many ways to increase devotion. The fact that you want to cultivate devotion is a most important thing. Sometimes we can be satisfied with where we are, but devotion has a sense of movement – getting closer to the Master, giving up our old self. It is not like you join the Ashram and spend the first three months learning everything you need to learn. No, with real devotion, there is no end to the Master's path – it is an eternal journey.

"What about fanatical devotion?" asked Donald.

"A fanatical devotion is usually driven by some kind of ego or stubbornness. There is an illumining story from the Mahabharata. Arjuna and Sri Krishna walk past an ascetic who is eating dried grass, but who also carries a sword by his side. Without revealing his identity, Arjuna asks the ascetic why he carries a sword by his side. The ascetic replies that he is a very devoted follower of Sri Krishna, but he also wishes to kill four devotees of Krishna because they pray to Krishna and take up his time. The ascetic goes on to say if he ever meets that rascal Arjuna, he will kill him. Why? Because Arjuna had the audacity to ask Lord Krishna to be his charioteer.

"Now, this kind of fanaticism has nothing to do with real devotion. Perhaps the ascetic had an unconscious feeling of jealousy that other people were outwardly close to Sri Krishna, and what he really wanted was to have that physical closeness himself.

"Real devotion means we are willing to serve the Master in

his own way. Suppose the Master asks us to get him a glass of Coca-Cola. A real devotee will immediately get it. But it is possible our clever mind thinks, 'I am so devoted. I have to protect my Master's health, so I will get him a glass of water instead. That is what the Master really wants.' Or perhaps we think, 'Only one glass of cola? I need to do something much more spectacular to show my devotion.' So we spend more money to get a Coca-Cola, plus take time to buy an expensive glass to serve it in. The Master will always try and appreciate our devotion, but he would be much more pleased if we just did what he asked immediately, and not waste the Master's time by trying to impress with something the Master didn't need.

"Real devotion is doing what the Master wants in his own way. False devotion is doing what we would like to give the Master. Look at the poor ascetic. He thinks Krishna wants to be left alone, but how does he know? Do not spiritual Masters gain great satisfaction from serving the world and their disciples? Was Krishna not overjoyed when Arjuna declined Krishna's vast armies but requested Krishna to be his charioteer during the battle of Kurukshetra?

"If the ascetic was really unsure, he could have asked Krishna for guidance, and Krishna would have illumined him and said, 'Of course, I don't want you to kill my dearest disciples! Meditate on love – not jealousy and hate!' But because the ascetic was so consumed with jealousy and anger, he couldn't even recognise Krishna when he appeared in person.

"It sounds like that ascetic should have listened to the advice of Swami Vivekananda – that he would make more progress playing football," said Donald.

"Yes!" said Bahir. "If you live a balanced life, you don't get the same fanatical and unbalanced ideas. Sometimes you read stories about the Cosmic gods and great sages meditating for thousands of years just to gain the occult power to destroy their enemies. What a waste of a few thousand years!

"Another example," said Bahir. "The Master liked us to speak and share his philosophy. If we are devoted to the Master, we will feel this is as important as our own personal meditation. But we have to do this with humility. If we see someone is not interested or not receptive, there is nothing to be gained by insisting they listen. We are not trying to proselytise. Real devotion means we will be patient and wait for the right time and place. A fanatical devotion will say, 'I am going to spread the Master's philosophy even if people don't want to hear, or if it is not the right time.' But then – if we proceed like a bull in a China shop – we only cause problems for the Master. If our devotion is causing problems for the Master, how can this be real devotion?

"One other thing: it is not always immediately obvious what is true devotion and false devotion. Sri Ramakrishna once asked for a Tulsi fruit out of season. Even the great disciples of Sri Ramakrishna thought it impossible. But Nag Mahasay went, and after three days, he did the impossible and found it. The other disciples of Sri Ramakrishna didn't share Nag Mahasay's faith. If you didn't have the faith of Nag Mahasay perhaps you would have gone out, and after two days of fruitless searching, become discouraged and gone back resentful – thinking that the Master had wasted your time. But Nag Mahasay had the faith to stay at the task until the end.

"Nag Mahasay was a very advanced seeker. When he got prasad on a banana leaf, he would start to eat the banana leaf, because he saw it as all coming from the Master. His brother disciples would try and snatch away the banana leaf before he could eat it. The thing is, if we eat a banana leaf – thinking we are showing our devotion – we just get stomach ache. Nag Mahasay had the absorption in the Master's consciousness that is very rare, so he was able to do it without getting stomach ache. For one disciple an action may be real devotion, but if we try to replicate the same physical action, it can become false devotion because we are not doing the action from the same inner level of consciousness and surrender.

"There is a story from the Mahabharata about the greatest devotee of all – Hanuman. Hanuman had such faith that by repeating the name of Rama he could walk on water. Now another person on the riverbank saw Hanuman walking on water and wanted to do the same thing. So Hanuman told the person to close his eyes and then he gave him a piece of paper with the name of Rama written on it. Then Hanuman said, 'Hold this piece of paper, but don't look at it until we get to the other side.' So the man takes the paper and is overjoyed to see he can miraculously walk on water. But, halfway across, he becomes curious to read the paper. So he takes it out and reads. He is shocked to see that the paper only says 'Rama'. But as he reads the word Rama and laughs, he loses the ability to walk on water and he drowns. Hanuman had a living faith in Rama – a devotion he had developed over a long time. The man didn't have the same faith in Rama, so he couldn't repeat the feat of Hanuman."

"So as a beginner seeker we shouldn't try walking on water," said Donald.

"Exactly, don't run before you can walk!" said Bahir.

"Sometimes," said Donald, "I see disciples stick to the letter of the Master's request and it can seem an anachronism in this modern world. How do we know if this is real devotion or false devotion?"

"Who knows? It is a good question. One thing I would say if a disciple is sincerely trying to listen to the requests of the Master, is don't ever criticise or put obstacles in their path. We shouldn't judge by the standards of the world – they are always changing. How much the world has changed in 20-30 years – it is unbelievable. But the world will continue to change its values and standards. The Master's teachings are eternal – not for a particular decade or fashion. Maybe there is an inner reason why the Master gave a particular piece of advice, which may not be immediately obvious from a worldly perspective. Quite often the Master didn't approve of shortcuts, but wanted us to exercise some deeper level of aspiration. Now if we feel the necessity of taking a shortcut, that is our decision, but we should definitely allow others to make their own choices and stick to what the Master said. If we follow the Master in every regard, this may have an inner value that is hard for the human mind to comprehend.

"If there is one thing I have learnt from 60 years of following the spiritual life, it is that the Master is always right. Now that may sound like fanatical devotion. But it is not a glib statement. It is something I have learnt from innumerable life experiences. Quite often I have followed my own wisdom, but at a later date, realised why the Master had a particular philosophy or said something different. It has happened so many times, even my mind has come to the conclusion the Master is always right. At the same time, I know how hard it is to live up to the highest ideals of the Master. A fanatical devotion wants to force the Master's wisdom on everyone else, but real devotion is concerned with our own attitude, and not the devotion of others.

"Now, Donald. I hear the Master's favourite food is pizza and ice cream, so perhaps it is time to go and show our outer devotion."

"Yes. Excellent idea. I like this kind of devotion!" said Donald.

WHAT'S UP?

"What's up Donald? It's not like you to be so quiet." asked Bahir.

"Well it seems Bob doesn't like me anymore," said Donald.

"Hmm, maybe not. Let's not rush to conclusions. I'll tell you something Gopal mentioned many years ago. Gopal felt someone was treating him badly and he happened to mention this to the Master. The Master smiled compassionately and said,

'Don't take it personally. When people have frustrations, it can appear they take them out on others. What you are seeing is jealousy and insecurity, but these are universal forces. I know how much devotion Tom has for me. A seeker can be both very devoted but still subject to these universal forces of ignorance.'"

"We are all work in progress," said Donald.

"Yes," said Bahir. "When people exhibit these emotions, it helps to not take it too personally. We are all struggling through life the best we can. The Master also told Gopal that if someone feels badly treated, they tend to react in two ways – they may retreat or they try to make the other person feel bad. In my case, when problems come up, sometimes I take it as an excuse to retreat. But the Master says the real solution is to develop oneness. If our left arm is weaker than our right arm, we don't get mad at the left arm, but we try to make it stronger. If someone is mean, it suggests they are unhappy. We shouldn't add to their unhappiness, but maintain our own cheerfulness.

"The Master once said something quite striking: if we don't resolve difficult issues in this incarnation, they will come back more strongly in future incarnations."

"You mean we will end up living with the same people we don't get on with?" said Donald.

"Yes! There is no escape! I heard one Master say that if you harbour hate for a particular nation, you may find in your next incarnation you are born in the very nation that you hated in your last life. The thing is that while we can see problems to be avoided, to the soul they are an opportunity to change something in our nature; an opportunity to learn a lesson that strengthens our inner character.

"But, going back to the situation with Bob, I would like to pass on a lesson that I have experienced many times over the years. The mind expects the worst, but the heart sees and feels the best in other people. You worry Tom thinks ill of you, but I bet you are wrong. Don't place too much emphasis on recent events.

"Now since the Master's passing, I sometimes see aspects of the Master's path in different ways to the ways my friend does. It's not really disagreement, it's just that we place a different value on different aspects. Now, in one frame of mind, we can think, 'I'm right and he's wrong. And never the twain shall meet.' But this is not a helpful way of looking at the situation; just because we see life in a different way, doesn't mean we can't get on very well. It's a mistake to be intolerant of situations where people see things differently or have different personalities. Look at how the Master managed so many 'interesting' situations amongst the disciples. He was trying to juggle our different expectations and demands, but even if we severely disappointed him, he was still offering his unconditional love. If the Master demanded and tolerated only the highest standards in the Ashram, would anyone be left?"

"So what should I do?" said Donald.

"I don't know," said Bahir. "Advice is cheap to give. Everyone wants to give advice – especially those who need it most! But since you've asked, maybe you don't need to do very much at all. Things have a habit of working out. Don't hold onto unfortunate experiences, and never overvalue the negative judgements of the mind."

"Yes. I like giving advice too," said Donald.

"So what advice would you give to an old man like me, Donald?" said Bahir.

"I think you should come to my ice-cream parlour more often," said Donald.

"See! We should swap jobs. You should be the philosopher and I can be the ice-cream eater. That would probably solve us both a lot of our problems!"

Bahir continued, "Quite a few times, I felt people were negative in their perception of me – especially when I rarely saw them or spoke to them in person. But, when I met them, I realised the mind had magnified something that wasn't really there. That's why it's important to keep in touch. Actually speaking to people is under-rated these days, but it can help maintain healthy relationships.

"I'll tell you a short story," said Bahir. "Where I used to work, I used to like to keep my office very clean. But as soon as I cleaned the office, a fellow worker would – as if by magic – leave a dirty pot. As soon as I cleaned, the dirt reappeared. The thing is that sometimes my mind would say, 'He's doing it just to annoy me. He knows I like it clean, but I get the opposite.' But I realised this is wrong. It wasn't actually a personal thing. I learned it's partly the operation of these universal forces."

"You mean lethargy and laziness," said Donald.

"Maybe. But also I think pride. When someone tells us what to do, our pride comes forward and we think or say, 'I won't be told what to do!'"

"Sometimes when people tell me what to do," said Donald, "I make a point of doing the opposite!"

"Yes. That can happen!" said Bahir.

"Also, another idea of mine," continued Bahir, "in our subconscious nature we are influenced by our past incarnations. Some boys I see and I secretly wonder to myself whether in their past incarnation they had servants or a wife to pick things up after them! Now as our Master would say, 'cock and bull story.' One disciple in a previous incarnation had been a king. And in this incarnation – maybe it is my imagination –perhaps you could see some regal habits and regal presumptions hanging over into his worldview. He acted as if servants would do his work and clean up after him. He was the big shot, but he took for granted that others would tidy up after him and do the less glamorous jobs. At the same time, another disciple – perhaps he had also been someone very significant in the past too, but in this incarnation it was all humility. So the point is that we have to transcend our entrenched habits and thought patterns of the past."

"I like the story you told me a while back, that the Master said sometimes young souls were easier to mould in the spiritual life because they didn't have the same baggage and entrenched ideas as old souls who have had hundreds of incarnations."

"Did I tell that story?" asked Bahir, "I can't remember telling that or where I got that from! But whether true or not, flexibility, tolerance and willingness to change are really important in the spiritual life."

"Yes, as I say," said Donald, "you have to empty the bowl completely, to be able to fill it up with new ice cream!"

MAINTAINING STANDARDS

With a degree of hesitation, Alex said, "There was one thing I wanted to ask you, Bahir."

"Sure," said Bahir.

"Well, when the Ashram meditates together, the Master stipulated certain standards. For want of a better example, he asked us to wear white clothing. But as leader of a local Ashram, what do you do if someone wears a cream top or white with black stripes? On the one hand, I want us to live up to the Master's standards. But on the other hand, I don't want to go around and tell people their clothing is not as white as it should be. I don't want to diminish the good, harmonious feeling we have and become too pernickety."

"Alex, I appreciate your sincerity. You have really encapsulated a dilemma. When I had responsibility for our local Ashram, I wrestled with this dilemma for many years. It took me 70 years of carefully weighing up the issue – with all its nuances and subtlety – until I was finally able to solve it."

There was a pause, and so Alex said, "Well, please do share it."

"Well, my dear Alex, the solution was that I retired and handed responsibility over to you!"

Bahir laughed vigorously and looked very pleased with himself. Alex looked a bit non-plussed.

"Sorry, Alex. I couldn't resist. In truth, there are different ways to answer this question. I'm not quite sure how to start. But I remember our Master once said that when his disciples walk past him during meditation, he does not see our outer imperfections. He sees instead the living presence of the Supreme Himself. In the Master's highest Transcendental consciousness, he sees and feels the underlying unity and oneness of creation. In this state of realisation, everything appears as a manifestation of God. We cannot imagine, but this is the realisation of all the great spiritual Masters.

"Now our Master can live and operate on several planes of consciousness at once. He did not just remain in the highest samadhi trance. He could fly from the physical plane to nirvana and back – all within a fleeting moment. When the Master asked us to pay attention to the outer physical – cleanliness, purity, tidiness – he was simultaneously seeing the God within. If we don't bathe or we wear the wrong clothes, in no way does it affect the realisation of the Master. But the Master knew that this realisation his disciples did not have. If we make effort with our appearance – to be clean, modest – it adds to the collective aspiration. But if during meditation we wear striking, immodest clothes, we are subtly drawing attention to ourselves. Equally in meditation, if we fidget, make noise or start talking, we are creating an outer disturbance that makes it harder for others. If we really value oneness, we will feel the importance of listening to the Master and will try to follow his requests. Otherwise, we are making the spiritual life a little more difficult for others – and of course more difficult for ourselves.

"Now the question comes – how do you respond? Once somebody complained to the Master about the clothes people were wearing. How did the Master respond? He said, 'Yes, I want disciples to wear dignified and modest clothing, but you have to go beyond complaining. Focus on your meditation, your inner silence, and don't get caught by eyeing up the outer imperfection of others.'"

Alex said, "I know what you mean. When I'm in a bad mood, I notice these little things more, and they annoy me. But then I don't want to say anything, because if I speak with frustration it will make it worse. I want to encourage higher standards, but who wants to be scolded by an old misery guts? But when I'm in a good consciousness, I don't get bothered by these little things and, at the same time, I feel I could say the right thing in a constructive, sympathetic way."

Bahir smiled, "There is a lot of wisdom in that. One other story I will mention. When I go to some retreats, I really enjoy the evening functions. I feel the very solid presence of the Master and get absorbed in meditating on the heart. In my own way, I think I am meditating well. Perhaps it is just wishful thinking, but after a soulful performance I want to maintain that feeling of silence and continue to meditate. But I notice as soon as the performance stops, some other people start chatting.

"It is a little disturbing to my efforts at meditation, but at the same time, I sail in the boat of not saying anything. I suffer in silence! Who wants to be the one asking people to be quiet? At the same time, there are other people who – God bless them – do sometimes speak nicely and say, 'Please be quiet.' Inwardly I am offering these people my gratitude like anything. So here is the proof ¬¬– if we remind people to respect sacred places and periods of meditation, it is a real service to many disciples.

"But always we have to use wisdom. There are times for soulfulness and seriousness and there are times for chatting and joy. We have to be careful about getting hung up on certain standards. We all have our outer foibles and habits, but if we feel someone's big heart, how much other things can pale into insignificance. At the same time, Alex, it is a sign of your oneness with the Master that you do value everything he says – even the so-called 'little' things which actually are not 'little' at all. In the Master's eyes, there is no such thing as insignificant disobedience. But how many people can you say this to?

"Another story. Many thousands of years ago, there was a spiritual Guru who was disheartened by his disciple's constant disobedience, so he said, 'From now on you must report the disobedience of your disciple friends to me. Outwardly, your friends may not like it, but inwardly their soul will be very grateful.' Now after two weeks, the Master with a sad face said, 'No. It is too much! I am absolutely inundated with complaints. From now on, I have a new philosophy. My new philosophy is: for God's sake, mind your own business!'

"What can I say? The spiritual life is not black and white – you have to use your wisdom. In your case it is a little different as you have some responsibility for our local Ashram – in a loving and compassionate way, it is necessary for you to care for the Master's standards. Sometimes outwardly others may seem to resent your caring for these standards, but we have to remember we belong only to our Master."

"What about the Master," asked Alex. "How strict was he when he was in the physical?"

"Well that's a good question, and I fear I will not be able to do justice to your question. If you asked Chetan he may say one thing, and if you asked Abhik he might say something else. For what it is worth, I feel the Master embodies the strictest standards and a degree of tolerance – all at the same time.

"The Master spoke about so many different things at so many different times to so many different people. Often the Master would answer the same question differently depending on who was asking the question! So you might conclude that the Master changed his standards. No! His answers were directed to the inner needs of the seeker who was asking the question!

"We have to remember that the Master only wanted our liberation. Furthermore, because he had travelled the long path of realisation, he could clearly see how we could expedite our own journey. The Master gave us divine wisdom on so many of the smallest details. We are so lucky to have a Master who lived for a considerable time and offered so much invaluable spiritual wisdom. But, at the same time, he definitely didn't want to make a religion of rules. We will never become a monastery where there are strict rules about how you eat, walk, speak e.t.c."

"Yes. Thank God!" said Alex.

"Though," said Bahir with a grin on his face, "perhaps I know one or two people who would benefit from a day of silence once a week!"

"But more seriously," said Bahir, "I remember that the Master once asked my old friend Jahangir to start an Ashram in a new country. The Master said to Jahangir – when you start the Ashram – I would like you to be strict right from the start. Please keep the highest standards right from the beginning. Years later, when I once visited the Ashram in that country, it was very inspiring. You really felt an added clarity, purity and luminosity. Now some of those Ashram members would tease the strict Jahangir saying he was a hard taskmaster, but the teasing was done with affection. Jahangir set high standards, but it wasn't about austerity and permanent seriousness. The Ashram aspired to higher standards while also keeping the joie de vivre – which is the essence of a spiritual community."

Alex leaned forward and said, "If I had to choose between an Ashram which was all rules, seriousness and rigidity, and the opposite, I would probably choose the Ashram with greater tolerance. You have to start with joy and happiness – otherwise what use is a long list of rules?"

Bahir replied, "Yes. I would probably make the same choice. But, at the same time, I feel it is a mistake to feel the two are mutually exclusive – I would say the opposite. Aspiring to high standards is ultimately the best way to increase our inner joy. The Master once said that in the future, there will be Ashrams which will combine the sweetest oneness with the strictest discipline. When you have that sweetest oneness, discipline comes spontaneously – not as a forced discipline."

Alex added, "It is interesting the Master asked Jahangir to set high standards by starting a completely new Ashram without any old disciples. When people are set in certain ways of living and behaving, it can be hard to get them to change tracks."

Bahir smiled, "Alex, this is the proof – how well you are learning to speak diplomatically these days. I know what you mean and can read between the lines!"

"Yes, in the old days, I might have called a spade a spade and then got into hot water soon after," said Alex.

"Yes, here is the Master's wisdom – don't cause waves unless it is necessary. But also you make quite a perceptive point. When we get into bad habits and spend 20 or 30 years doing them, we stop thinking they are bad habits – we can start to feel we are actually doing the right thing. Here I am not talking about anyone else – only myself. The mind is a miracle of self-justification. Whatever we do, the mind can twist reality until it believes it is doing absolutely the right thing.

"In the Master's case, he was acutely aware of human nature, and what was possible and what was not. When a pattern of behaviour is well entrenched, the Master may have to tolerate it – because he is looking at the bigger picture. Spiritual transformation is challenging – we can't change all aspects of our nature all at once. If the branch doesn't bend in the wind, it will snap completely. So, similarly, sometimes we need to bend with the wind when dealing with human nature.

"But with a completely new Ashram, perhaps the Master saw the potential to create something new – something where old habits were not engrained. If you want new disciples to aspire to high standards, the first thing they will do is look around to see what old disciples are doing. If we are sleeping and snoring, how can we expect new disciples to live up to the Master's very highest standards? And it is important to remember the Master did set high standards. During meditation, especially those who sat on the front row, he stipulated they should sit attentively; immaculate white clothing; feet flat on the floor; no slouching or crossing of legs. And if he was here today, I'm sure he'd add, 'No fiddling with your phones!' The reason is the physical reflects the mental attitude. If we want to have a devoted attitude, we have to at least start with the physical. If we cross our legs and slouch in the chair, it gives off the wrong vibration. But, if we sit properly, attentively, then it is easier for the mind and heart to follow suit."

Alex replied, "Yes, but it is a rare soul who can maintain high standards and also be joyful at the same time."

"I fully agree," said Bahir, "but I can also see you are one of those rare souls. I have faith that you will do an excellent job looking after our little Ashram."

"Bahir, you're always very good with the flattery! But it's one thing to have good intentions – it's another to be able to implement them."

"Don't feel it is you who are doing it. Feel you are just the instrument. Also, if there is one thing I would add, Alex: always start with your own spiritual life. Aspire, meditate and cultivate joy. Set standards in your own life. Only when you have reached a degree of joy and detachment should you worry about what others are doing. And never forget that it is not your responsibility. It is the Master's – it is God's responsibility. It is just occasionally the Master needs a few willing instruments to help inspire others."

"Well, Bahir. We are no closer to knowing what to do on specific issues. But I suppose it's good to know others wrestle with the same issue."

"One final thing, Alex. I do believe in reincarnation. Well actually I really hope so – because this incarnation is nearly up! Anyway, in either the near or distant future, I'm sure there will be Ashrams of absolutely the highest standard on both the inner and outer planes – and these will be veritably places of Heaven on earth. Perhaps in the future, disciples will look back and be amazed at our comparatively low standards, but we have to start from somewhere. A saint is just a sinner who never gave up!"

"Well, I am quite inspired by that thought," said Alex, "but, when you 'go upstairs' and enjoy your well-earned retirement, don't forget us down here. Perhaps from Heaven, you can exert a little influence on our little Ashram."

"Well, upstairs, I shall try not to forget how difficult the earth plane can be!"

APPRECIATION

"Alex our previous conversation reminds me of the other side of the coin. We can easily get caught up in following our own spiritual life, but it is important to make an effort to encourage and appreciate others."

"Well, before your time, I learned quite a few things from old Rohan, the previous leader of our local Ashram. Amongst many sterling qualities, one thing I always noticed. Sometimes, when someone in the Ashram would perform some small service, I thought it to be insignificant or I would find some minor fault with it. But Rohan had this very good quality of sincere appreciation. Naturally, it made people feel welcomed and appreciated. At that time, this quality I didn't have. I came from a culture which was quite reserved. Often I thought to myself, 'I would never have thought of appreciating the person like that,' but I could see it was done in a very positive spirit. And I think to myself, 'I'm glad Rohan is here to say something encouraging, because I would have missed the opportunity.'"

"Yes. I see that is a good quality, but I fear it can be difficult to know the right words," said Alex.

"I wouldn't worry about the right words. The important thing is the sincerity, and the fact you care to notice and appreciate. If we can be in that frame of mind – looking for good qualities in other people – it will definitely help everyone."

"What about the Master – how would he offer appreciation?" asked Alex.

"Well, that is an interesting one," said Bahir.

"I remember when I was a new disciple visiting the Master for the first time. The Master would often smile and speak to older disciples – perhaps appreciating something they had done. So I expected the same. But often when I walked past the Master, he would close his eyes and look away. I never got that outer recognition and the outer contact. I was a little bemused – put out, perhaps – and this continued for quite a few years. I took this as the Master's inner teaching – that he wanted me to look within for his appreciation and love, and not rely on outer signs. When I had learnt this lesson and no longer expected anything from the Master, he then started to offer the occasional smile and look directly into my eyes. These were blessingful moments I remember and cherish. But then, when the Master passed behind the curtain of Eternity, I was ready. I knew the real Master was the inner connection, the inner source – not these outer signs, as beautiful as they were.

"The Master definitely did offer the most sincere encouragement and appreciation, and it was always done with a spirit that inspired you to go on and do more. I heard many times the Master appreciate like anything the achievement of disciples, but there was never a sense of completion or fulfilment. The Master always saw a divine achievement as the first stepping stone to something greater. If you put on a concert for 500 people, the Master would appreciate and offer gratitude, but at the same time he would say, 'Very good, but could you not get 1,000 people next time?' Once the Master rang up my friend Anil and said, 'Anil, I am very pleased with you – but, now, I wish you to please me infinitely more.'

"I also heard from old Chetan that the Master would say when he praised his disciples it could also cause problems. Perhaps the individual would be bloated with pride or develop a sense of complacency. At the same time, the Master said when he praised disciples it was often very helpful for other disciples who were present, and they received inspiration from the Master's praise. Again, the Master emphasised that the absolute best service is that done without any expectation of outer acknowledgement. It is a reminder that to receive praise in the right spirit is also a challenge.

"I remember one occasion when a group of boys completed a remarkable achievement of reciting 1,000 of the Master's poems by heart. The Master appreciated their achievement like anything. But interestingly the Master also asked other groups of disciples to offer their own congratulations and gifts to this group. Now, the Master never said why – so this is only my understanding – but I wonder if the Master was getting the whole Ashram to offer their appreciation so there would be no room for jealousy. Because we were following the Master's request and taking time to offer appreciation, everybody could feel their oneness with this significant achievement.

"This is why it is good to offer appreciation and encouragement. It not only inspires the other person, but also brings to the fore our divine qualities and edges out the bad qualities of jealousy and insecurity.

"Going back to our local Ashram, it is good to take time to appreciate those disciples who are perhaps quieter. Some disciples naturally fill the limelight because they are very talented and outwardly successful. But if you look around, there are many people quietly doing small things, which can be easy to take for granted. Now, if we were all realised souls, we would not need any encouragement or appreciation. But none of us are realised souls – which is why we come to the Ashram. Appreciation doesn't have to be a big show. Even just taking the time to notice can make a big difference.

"Also, I would even go further. Try to create a situation which gives you the opportunity to bring to the fore the good qualities of other people. I remember when some new disciples joined a local Ashram run by Sunil. These disciples had interest in the creative arts – writing, poetry. So Sunil set up an evening, once a month, where the disciples meditated and then tried to produce creative work. Sunil was creating an opportunity to bring others to the fore. I feel the Master would like very much the spirit of this. It is the flexibility to create a situation where you can allow others to shine. It shows we care and want to create a family feeling."

"It's certainly more fun than scolding others for failing to meet certain standards," said Alex with a smile.

"Yes, absolutely," said Bahir. "I'm not saying you can achieve everything by appreciation alone, but you can definitely help steer the boat in the right direction. Also, if you are always noticing the bad qualities or imperfections of other disciples, maybe the problem is actually within yourself. If you find one member of the Ashram is not doing well, and you're frustrated with them, go out of your way to try and see some of their divine qualities. The Master said that no matter how badly a disciple was doing, often when he thought about them their one good quality would come to the fore and that outweighed all their imperfections."

"It is very good what you say," said Alex, "but sometimes I find it difficult to appreciate. Like you, I came from a culture where the closest you get to appreciating a friend is a gentle punch in the stomach and a back-handed compliment – like 'nice one, fat-so!'"

"Yes! I know there is a hidden affection in our regional teasing! But, sometimes these things don't translate well to other cultures. And, of course, physical contact is always inappropriate. But you don't have to imitate the over-the-top superlatives of our wonderful cousins across the pond. That is too much for me too; it's just a cultural thing. The important thing is sincerity. And quite often what people crave is not praise, but just recognition. Don't wait for people to fish for compliments. Look around! Even a simple word can make a difference. And don't take anyone for granted.

"For me, it was a long learning curve. Ironically, I spent a good 10-20 years inwardly appreciating the way older disciples could appreciate and encourage. And as I always say – if you sincerely encourage the divine qualities of others, eventually those qualities rub off on you.

"Of course, it was always interesting being at functions with the Master. In the majority of cases, the Master would not say anything outwardly – the Master spoke in silence – but, the Master would also often surprise. I remember one musical performance. It dragged on for a long time and, frankly, it was not so good! Here I am being diplomatic! Eventually, it comes to an end and I breathe a sigh of relief. But how does the Master respond? He jumps up and gives the most enthusiastic praise and encouragement. Now I start to feel a little guilty. If my Master likes something, I also want to like it out of oneness, So I try to quieten my previous thoughts. But we can never know the inner reasons for the Master's actions. For example, once the Master was keeping a particular disciple very close to him – giving him many wonderful opportunities for personal service. And if the disciple did anything good, the Master would praise him like anything. Then after a few months of this special treatment, this disciple just left the Ashram. I later heard via Chetan that the Master had said he knew this disciple was thinking of leaving the Ashram, so the Master was doing everything to try and keep him connected to the spiritual life. The Master would try so hard to keep people in the spiritual life – even if it was at great personal cost to his own manifestation. It seemed nothing came close to the Master's care and concern for our own spiritual life.

"Yet, if some disciple was doing very well in the spiritual

life, the Master may go to the other extreme and outwardly ignore them because they are ready for the higher teaching of developing an inner connection. So the outer praise could serve many functions. The Master always had inner reasons for acting the way he did, which were not always logical to our rational mind."

'GURU SAID', PART 1

Donald spoke to Bahir, "Often I hear disciples say, 'Guru said XYZ.' To what extent should we trust this aural remembrance?"

Bahir replied, "That is a good question. And to answer, perhaps I could relate a few stories from the hoary past.

"Many years ago there was a spiritual Master who spent considerable time meditating in silence. Sometimes the Master gave talks to the whole Ashram, and at other times he would give messages to particular disciples, who were then responsible for passing the message on to everyone else.

"The Master was often very serious about the spiritual life, but to help his disciples relax, he could also slip into a light-hearted mood, where he would cut jokes and talk about juicy topics. On one occasion, a major newspaper had published a cynical article about yoga, which had disturbed some of the disciples. A reporter, with little sympathy to the subject, had distorted the real meaning of yoga, but exaggerated the misdeeds of a fake guru who had become enamoured with ostentatious displays of material wealth. Although the story contained some truths, it tarnished all practitioners of yoga with the same brush. Some disciples expressed concern to the Master – saying this may make it difficult for the Ashram's manifestation in town. The Master looked unperturbed, revealing his infinite poise and detachment. Dismissively, the Master said, 'It shows you can never believe anything you read in a newspaper.'

"The disciples asked the Master if they should contact the paper to try and correct the mistruths in the article. The Master went silent for a moment and then replied, 'No. In this case, it is best to concentrate only on getting good, positive articles in print. Let us ignore these wild falsehoods. Try to feel you are like an elephant and the world's criticism is nothing more than an insignificant ant. Instead, let us concentrate on trying to inspire the world with our cheerful self-offering.' The disciples were deeply inspired by the Master's wisdom, inner poise and faith in God's Plan. Their discouragement from reading the article soon dissipated in the presence of the Master.

"The next day, the small number of disciples who were with the Master that night made an effort to share the Master's conversation with the rest of the Ashram. Other disciples gained tremendous inspiration from the Master's talk – even though it was related second-hand.

"However, as stories got passed around the Ashram, some disciples remembered or emphasised particular aspects of the Master's talk. A few disciples really concentrated on the Master's phrase, 'You can't trust anything you read in a newspaper.'

As a result, whenever they read news, they would believe the opposite. They would say, 'It's all a conspiracy, the real truth is something completely different!' When some pointed out another opinion, they would say, 'But the Master said we should never trust anything written in a newspaper.'

"Other disciples who were with the Master that evening said, 'You are taking it out of context. The Master's phrase came during a long conversation in response to a particular incident. It would be a mistake to take it as a generalisation.'

"Another disciple said, 'The Master has also said we should be careful of becoming drawn into the world of current affairs and political debate. If our mind is full of news, judgement, and strong opinion, it will leave no space for the peace and joy the Master is trying to bring down.'

"This went on for a few months, but later there was a report in the newspaper that citizens were advised to take a vaccination against a new virus sweeping the area. The news created different opinions in the Ashram. Some felt it was an important duty; others felt it was just cynical forces creating unnecessary fear in society. The news was reported to the Master, who took the report very seriously. He asked one of his doctor disciples to speak directly to the chief medical officer in the government. He was able to ascertain it was a real threat and an inoculation was desirable. As a result, the Master asked his disciples to follow the advice of local government and get an inoculation.

"Later that day, the Master invited questions from his disciples. One disciple asked, 'Master, I thought you said we should never trust anything we read in the paper?' "

The Master looked bemused and said, 'Did I say that?' Then he laughed and said, 'Perhaps I did in conversation, but you have to use your wisdom. It is certainly advisable to retain a critical eye of what you read in newspapers. Often they publish distortions if not outright lies. But it is absurd to go to the other extreme and believe everything is false.'

"The Master continued, 'Unfortunately, I can see that some disciples are becoming too immersed in the political world. By seeing all the bad news and assuming everything is some kind of conspiracy or bad motivation, you are really poisoning your own spiritual life. As a spiritual seeker, your only responsibility is to pray, meditate and see the beauty in life. The moon has dark spots, true, but let us concentrate on its soulful beauty. If you read a paper only to become indignant at the falsehoods embedded in them, your consciousness will be little better than the person writing it. If you are immersed in the world of divisive argument, it will affect your own outlook on life more than you can ever imagine. So do not worry about affairs over which you have no control. Instead, let us do our little bit to try and bring about Heaven on earth.'

"There was a pause and the Master said with a smile, 'Very good. Now is there anything else I might have said, which is causing confusion?'

"There was a little laughter from the disciples. But a disciple got up and said, 'Master, today you asked to be inoculated with allopathic medicine. But I thought you once said allopathic medicine is deeply flawed.'

"The Master paused and said, 'Let me tell you a short story.

Once there was a very devout religious person who was caught up in a serious flood. He only escaped by climbing onto the roof of his house. He began to intensely pray to God to save him. After a few hours of non-stop prayer, a rickety old boat came by the house and the boatman said, 'Come, get in the boat. I will take you to safety.' The man said, 'Thank you but it is OK, I am praying to God. God will definitely answer my prayer and come to rescue me soon.' The boatman looked perplexed but thought he wouldn't waste time with this madman so he rowed away. A few hours later, a helicopter came to his rescue, but the same thing happened. The man said, 'No thanks. Don't worry, God will soon come to save me.' The helicopter flew away.

Alas, in a few hours, the floodwater rose and the man drowned. The man found himself in Heaven, in front of St Peter. The religious man asked St Peter, 'How come I prayed so intensely but God didn't come to save me from drowning?' St Peter said, 'Goodness me! Who do you think it was who sent the boat and the helicopter if not God? The problem is you wanted to be saved in your own way, but you failed to see God was acting in and through the old boatman and helicopter rescue."

"The Master paused and then said, 'We have to know that allopathic medicine is very often the instrument God uses to cure us of poor health. Now it is true, Western medicine does not have all the answers. From one perspective some drug treatments are primitive to say the least. However, for some aspects of health, allopathic medicine is most effective. In the past 200 years, how many infectious diseases have been curtailed? Is this not God acting in and through the scientists and doctors?

"'Now it is also true that if you are highly advanced in yoga, there are ways to cure yourself through yoga and meditation. But I wish to say I do not have a single disciple who has that capacity. I'm not trying to discourage you. But if you are learning the ABCs, don't think you can jump straight to a Master's degree.

"'Now also there is also something called faith. Some disciples have such faith in God's Healing Power. With this faith, it is considerably easier for God to work in and through the doctors. But if you are ill, please go and see a doctor. What a headache it causes me when you stay home and suffer from your illness.'

"The Master looked most serious, but then he allowed himself a smile. 'Very good! Anything else this Master may have said!'

"A disciple got up and said, 'Master, I once heard that you said if we make a pilgrimage to the top of Mount Nero, we will need one less incarnation to realise God.'

"'Excellent! Let us all climb Mount Nero tomorrow! Perhaps the guides who climb Mount Nero every month are on the verge of realisation! It is like swimming in the Ganges. Our Indian scriptures say if you bathe in the Ganges all your sins are washed away. But what happens when you get out of the Ganges? All these sins immediately return because we haven't done the inner work to remove them from our consciousness. If you want to make a pilgrimage to Mount Nero, and you retain the highest consciousness of soulful gratitude, perhaps you really can burn off karma and expedite your spiritual journey. But if you mechanically walk to the top, there will be virtually zero spiritual benefit. It is always the inner attitude that is important. As you know, I encourage disciples with the capacity to make a pilgrimage, but do not think in mathematical terms of how much karma you will lose. Try to do the pilgrimage with as much soulfulness as you can and leave the results to God."

"'My children. If you want to understand my philosophy, read my books, listen to my tapes. It is all there. But be careful of making a religion out of a snatched phrase. Sometimes even spiritual Masters enjoy joking and speaking in a light-hearted manner. If we are serious all the time, it is too much. Use your wisdom to discriminate, and if still in doubt you can ask me. Is this all clear?' asked the Master.

"'Master,' said Paul, 'When you said I was your best disciple, does this mean you were not necessarily speaking from the absolutely highest plane of consciousness?'

"'Yes. Very good! I think I have several disciples who claim to be my 'best' disciple!'"

Note: this story was written in 2019

'GURU SAID', PART 2

Donald said, "So does that mean when people say, 'Guru said...,' I should never believe?"

Bahir replied, "Most of the time disciples are sincere in trying to share what Guru said. And you will be able to confirm in books, writings from other disciples. If it sounds a little fishy, by all means be cautious. However, sometimes the Master really did say something, but it can be a little inconvenient because we want to do something else! Then we say, 'Oh you can't trust anybody who recollects what the Master says.' But this just becomes a justification to do whatever we want. So, we have to avoid either extreme. We have to be very careful, both in putting words in the Master's lips, but also in arguing that the Master never meant what he did actually say.

"To help explain, perhaps I could share a story from the life of a spiritual Master, Swami Abhidananda, who lived many hundreds of years ago.

***

"Swami Abhidananda's Ashram was located between a city and a dense forest. There was a well-maintained road that went all the way around the forest, and it took one hour walk to get to the city. However, there was also a shortcut through the forest that took just 20 minutes. The path was quite interesting as it had religious shrines along the route. But also it could be dangerous, as bandits sometimes hid out in the forest and could assault passing travellers.

"After receiving a few disturbing reports from the forest, the Master said he no longer wanted his disciples to take the shortcut through the forest. Some disciples said to the Master, 'But Master, if we take the longer road we will have to shorten our evening lecture, because we will have less time.' The Master replied, 'That is fine, make them shorter if needed – your safety is more important than my manifestation.'

"The disciples listened to the new request of the Master and avoided the shortcut when coming to the Ashram. However, after a few months, a close disciple of the Master, called Mark, spoke to the Master and said, 'With my important job in the city, it takes a long time to get to the Ashram and I end up coming late for the evening meditations. I have bought this new electronic pager, which can call for help if needed. So can you please give me an exception to come through the forest so I can spend more time at your feet? I will be very careful.'

"The Master was silent. He knew if he made an exception, other disciples would want an exception too. But he also knew that Mark had a strong will. Mark was asking in the strong expectation the Master would say yes. If the Master refused his close disciple, Mark may become angry at the Master, and then he would suffer.

"At this moment, in the soul's world, two spiritual Master friends came in their subtle form to visit Swami Abhidananda. The first yogi-friend was all sympathy and concern for the

Master. He said, 'You already have so many physical ailments from your disciple problems, you should let this disciple take a shortcut. Otherwise, I know you will end up taking his anger on yourself. You already have too much stomach ache!'

"However, the other Master was indignant at the situation. He said, 'Your disciples are disobedience incarnate. Look at their audacity! You give a clear command and now they make this emotional demand to give them special permission. You should use your divine authority and tell them that if they are more interested in finding shortcuts and disobeying you, they will have to leave the Ashram."

"The Master inwardly smiled at his yogi-friends. To the second Master, he said, 'My dear friend, have you forgotten what it is like to be on the earth plane? How I would love to follow your advice. But if I asked all my disobedient disciples to leave, there would be no one left in the Ashram, except perhaps my two dogs! True, all my problems would be solved, but fortunately or unfortunately my Lord Beloved Supreme wishes me to adopt infinite compassion, forgiveness and patience to my beginner disciples. I have no will of my own. If the Supreme asks me to indulge my disciples in the hope that one day they will develop real devotion and real obedience to please me in my own way, then I will gladly follow the will of my Inner Pilot. If I was as strict as my own Master was to me, I know it would break my disciples. On the earth plane, sometimes spiritual Masters have to be like the tree bending in the wind.'

"All this juicy conversation happened within a fraction of

an earthly second. And as Swami Abhidananda looked at his disciple, Mark, all he could see was his good qualities – his big heart and generous nature. These two good qualities overrode all the Master's disappointment. So he said to Mark, 'Yes, OK but please do not broadcast my exception to the rest of the Ashram, otherwise they will want exceptions too, and with other younger disciples I would worry even more for their safety.'

"A few months later a few disciples saw Mark coming out of the forest, and they were surprised to see him. They asked Mark, 'But I thought the Master said we were not allowed to take the shortcut through the forest?'

"Mark replied, 'No. It is fine. The Master said I was allowed. I was given permission. I told the Master that with this electronic pager, it is perfectly safe, and so he agreed with me.'

"Mark forgot the Master's actual intentions, but retained a little pride that he had been given an exception. Now, it soon spread through the Ashram that as long as you bought an electronic pager, it was fine to take the shortcut through the forest. So many disciples were happy to be able to take the shortcut, and only a few disciples maintained the long walk around the forest edge. These disciples sometimes felt a little left behind because they missed out on more activities, but they remembered well the Master's talk and vividly felt the Master's seriousness in not wanting disciples to use the shortcut. They assumed that the Master had his own reasons for allowing Mark to be an exception. Unless they heard directly from the Master, they would not take the shortcut.

"This situation went on for a few months, and the idea of taking the shortcut become almost second nature. Some began to feel this was actually what the Master really wanted, as they had more time for manifestation. However, one evening, two disciples – Arun and Talak – were taking the shortcut through the forest when, out of the blue, a gang of bandits appeared from the undergrowth. Immediately they reached for their electronic alarm, but alas, there was no signal. In the dense forest canopy, it was useless. They tried to shine a light, but it was like a drop in the ocean and was soon nullified by the ominous shadows of the forest, which now took on a much more menacing feeling.

"A bandit pulled out a knife and put it to the face of Arun. 'Give me your money!' the bandit hissed with menace. Arun and Talak were frightened. They could see in the bandit's eye that he would happily kill for fun.

"Arun replied, 'But we are spiritual pilgrims, we only carry a few coins.'

"The bandit replied, 'Rubbish! Maybe I need to remove a few fingers to help you remember where you keep your wealth!'

"Arun glanced towards Talak, but he looked just as petrified, so in desperation he started to pray most fervently to his Master, 'Master save me! save me!'

"The bandits were getting restless. One of them said, whilst brandishing his long knife, 'If they don't have any money, at least let us have some fun!' The gang of bandits hissed like a pack of feral wolves.

"But at that moment, in the far distance, there was a powerful roar – sounding like a lion. The roar grew louder and it echoed through the still of the forest. Suddenly the atmosphere changed – now it was the turn of the bandits to feel uneasy. It sounded like the powerful lion was getting closer and it was looking for prey. The arrogant aggression of the bandits vanished and fear covered their faces. Filled with fear, the ring-leader dropped his knife from Arun's face and they all fled into the night. The roar of the lion somehow did not cause the same fear to enter into the two disciples. It was as if the lion was on their side. They just felt tremendous relief to see the bandits flee, and once they were well out of sight, it was their turn to start running towards the Ashram.

"They arrived at the Ashram in a cold sweat, and their fear was still vivid on their faces. The whole incident was related to Swami Abhidananda, who heard it all in a stony silence. That evening, the Master entered the function room with a steely silence and serious expression. The disciples dared not joke or chatter but sat alert as if on tenterhooks. After a long silent meditation, Swami Abhidananda began to speak.

"'When a spiritual Master says anything, you have to feel there is a reason. You may not always know why a Master states something, but everything we say is for your spiritual benefit. If you feel you know better than your Master, then you can take responsibility for your own life. But if you follow my path, if you take me as your Guru, you have to feel the necessity of listening to what I say.

"'I am sure you all know the story of the Ramayana, where

Lakshmana draws a ring of protection for Sita. But Sita disobeyed and then she was kidnapped by Ravana. If you go beyond the Master's world, if you disobey the Master, you cannot always expect the Master's protection.

"'The reason I forbade the shortcut, is that inwardly I saw that taking the shortcut opens you to hostile forces. When you are in the spiritual life, how alert bad forces can be. If you disobey my injunctions, then you are opening yourself up to these bad forces. Now, this evening because two disciples took a shortcut, I had to use all my occult power to save them from mortal danger. I do this despite their disobedience. But why do you have to create problems for your Master? If you go off on your own path, the Supreme's protection may not always be there. If you follow my path, then it is my responsibility and I can take care of you in my own way. But if you think you know better, then you are responsible for your life. So please, no more shortcuts!"

"The disciples were silent and dared not speak. Later a disciple asked, 'But Master, didn't you give an exception to one disciple?'

Swami Abhidananda replied, 'Yes. That is true. But, you have to know you may have no idea why I gave that particular disciple an exception. In his case, I become responsible. But, you should not assume that just because I gave one person an exception, that will necessarily apply to you. You should never take it for granted.'

"'But Master,' asked another disciple, "when we took the

shortcut, we were able to spend more time in selfless service and meditation.'

"'Unfortunately, you have the wrong attitude,' said the Master. 'When it comes to selfless service, you have to feel you are doing it for the sake of your Master. If you take shortcuts so that you can feel you are doing more for the Master, this is not the case. If you disobey me in order to achieve more outwardly, then I cannot appreciate in the same way as a disciple who spends less time but does it all in my own way. Also, forgive me, but there is a saying: if you want something done, ask a busy person. It is not always true that if you have more time, you actually use it for selfless service and meditation. Some disciples take the shortcut only so they can spend more time gossiping with their friends. So, dear children, let us not take any more shortcuts!'"

BEYOND LIKES AND DISLIKES

Alex asked Bahir, "Sometimes I feel everybody in the Ashram is eager to take one course of action, but to me it doesn't feel right, or at least it doesn't give me any joy. Then I feel miserable. What should I do?"

Bahir replied, "There are many ways to answer this question, depending on the particular issue. But one example springs to mind from many years ago. Somebody had the idea to set up video conference with different Ashrams so we can be in touch during our meditation sessions. It is something that never happened when the Master was in the body, but perhaps the question never got asked.

"Now, my instinctive reaction is that I don't like it. I like to meditate, and chat with friends afterwards. Video calls on a big screen, performing to a camera and all that, is not my cup of tea. When I hear this idea, my only desire is to sit right at the back and hide behind a plant pot. But at the same time, if everyone is eager, I'm not keen to dampen enthusiasm. I don't want to say anything, so remain silent.

"Now, of course, if we have a strong personal preference, it will colour our belief in what the Master would say. If we enjoy getting up late, we remember how tolerant and forgiving the Master was. If we like cold showers at 4 in the morning, this is what the Master wanted too. Maybe I'm being a bit flippant, but as the saying goes: you can always find a sentence from the Bible to justify what you want.

"Anyway, it's not so much whether the Master would want it or not. Who knows? The problem is I don't share the enthusiasm for this idea, so I feel a little bit put out. And seeing everyone else's enthusiasm makes me think, 'What's wrong with me?' So I'm mulling this over in my mind, feeling a little out of place. But then something snaps and I say to myself, 'This is ridiculous! My dear brothers are just trying to do what they think is a good thing. How can I feel put out by such a small issue?' I decided something is wrong with my attitude.

"If the Master was in the body, maybe he would encourage this video conferencing; maybe he wouldn't. Personally, I doubt it. But I feel there is no value in sharing my opinion – it's better to let things go. The one certainty is the Master always said, 'Don't indulge the negative emotions – frustration, depression and so on.' So I say to myself in this situation, 'Perhaps the most important thing is to transcend my frustration, be happy and go beyond my personal likes and dislikes.' So I make an effort to change my perception of the issue. The important thing is oneness. Do you remember my story about putting socks on my ears?" asked Bahir.

"Not really," said Alex.

"For the full story," said Bahir, "You'll have to buy one of my old books, now probably out of print, but full of great stories!"

"They should definitely reprint it, Bahir," said Alex.

"Thank you! You're a good man, Alex!" said Bahir. "Anyway,

STORIES FROM THE SPIRITUAL LIFE, PART 2

to cut a long story short, our Ashram group had this idea to put socks on their ears for a particular music performance for our Master. Of course, I thought it was a silly idea – I still do, 80 years later! But I went along with the Ashram decision out of oneness. After the performance, the Master indicated he liked our oneness, and he gave a gentle ribbing to those who sat on the side-lines looking sensible. What I learned from that experience is that sometimes you please the Master much more by maintaining cheerful oneness than with a righteous disapproval.

"So, with this new thing of video conferencing, I ended up challenging myself – 'Can I go beyond my habitual responses and instinctive emotions?' Interestingly, I had just read a book – not by our Master, I should add – but one particular spiritual practice the author mentioned was a practice of going from one emotion to another like they are keys on a keyboard and you are the piano player in charge. Feel an emotion, then transform it into the divine opposite.

Now, perhaps it is a bad idea to invoke a negative emotion even for a second. But we don't need to invoke, they come throughout the day. When they come, we can practise detaching and transcending. Don't feel a helpless victim to the emotion, which comes from your vital, but instead transform it into something divine. If we can do this, we can go beyond the whims of our lower self. So, this becomes my challenge.

"Anyway, a few months later, after meditation we have arranged a video conference, and my heart sinks at the prospect. But then I remember my promise, and I try to detach and observe where this emotion is coming from. And I play a trick on myself. I offer a prayer to the Master, 'Master, if you don't like this, make it a technological failure. If it is OK with you, make it a smooth technological process. But if it does all run smoothly, then I will take it as if you are physically here, blessing the experience, and I will try to be in my best consciousness.'"

"So did the video work?" asked Alex.

"Yes. Without a flaw!" replied Bahir. "Now you can say it is a silly prayer. The Master has infinitely better things to do than breaking internet connections from Heaven, but the symbolic point is that I gave responsibility to the Master, and I'm not allowing myself to get stuck in a loop of resentment that things aren't quite as they should be from my personal perspective. We can all carry a long list of grievances about wrong things in the Ashram and with other disciples, and when we get to Heaven, the Master will say, 'Very good. I agree with you 100%. But why did you have to make yourself unhappy?' In Heaven there will always be divine beings who will agree with our point of view. But we have to live on earth, not wait for vindication in Heaven.

"When the Master was in the body, he had many flawed instruments. Which human is not flawed? So, sometimes we are working on a project and our human nature conflicts with the other personalities. Then we want to leave the project, but the Master says, 'Maybe you are right; other disciples are seriously flawed and I sympathise with your complaints. At the same time, who suffers when you take umbrage and stay at home? It is me – my Mission.' So the Master is saying you can't wait for things to be perfect. Perfection is doing our task cheerfully, whatever others are doing."

"So did you enjoy the experience of the video conference?" asked Alex.

"Well, it seems that I'm not so good at going beyond my personal likes and dislikes!" said Bahir. "But in a strange way, I felt the Master was happy with my attitude. I didn't dampen anyone else's enthusiasm. I even managed to fake a smile. I just let it be, stayed happy and I stopped worrying whether it is right or wrong. Over time, if it is really feeding the souls of disciples, it will continue to happen. If it is not what the Master wants, hopefully it will gradually fade away. In different circumstances, this might be quite a fun thing. It's 'not my cup of tea' but who knows?

"Why do you keep using the phrase 'not my cup of tea?'" said Alex.

"It's a light, non-confrontational way of saying I don't like it," said Bahir. "If you say, 'I don't like it' – it is quite strong, rigid and definite. But in this case, I don't want to make it such a black and white judgement. I feel the phrase 'not my cup of tea' perfectly sums up how I wish to express my feelings."

"Do you think it is possible to go beyond likes and dislikes?" asked Alex.

"To some extent," said Bahir. "It is a real challenge, that is for sure. But the Master himself was proof that it is possible. Always the Master was constantly having to go beyond his personal preferences. The Supreme would ask him to do something, and the human in the Master would immediately surrender to the Divine in the Master. In the spiritual life, we always have to try and see things from the Master's point of view. But it is very easy to conflate our personal likes with the Master's teachings.

"Sometimes emotions come irrationally. Too often we identify 100% with them – then they increase in power and we feel the emotion is who we are. But the thing we need to know is that emotions are fleeting. We can choose whether to let bad emotions go or not. Of course, practice is much harder than theory. I suppose that is why life gives so many opportunities for progress."

"Well, it's all very inspiring, but what did the Master really think about video conferencing during meditation sessions?" asked Alex with a cheeky smile.

"It can be exhausting always trying to think this kind of question. A while back, I did hear old Jahangir say the Master gave an answer to this particular question – or something very similar – and also the reasons for his decision, but that was many years ago. You can ask him. But one thing I would say is that there are some issues, where you feel you have to stand by the Master's path, the Master's philosophy – even if it is not popular and not always understood. If you inwardly feel something is wrong and this feeling is confirmed by what you read or heard from the Master's talks, you can feel grateful that you are still trying to see the spiritual life from the perspective of the Master. This inner closeness to the Master's will is everything in the spiritual life. Also, it is good to maintain harmony. But the spiritual life is not a democracy – just because a majority believe something, that doesn't prove it is the highest Truth. But if you are always thinking the Ashram is wrong, if you are always thinking other people are wrong, this is also a warning sign, and you have to ask yourself whether there is something wrong with your mind. We have to choose very carefully when to go with the flow and when to put a flag in the wind."

"Yes," said Alex, "but sometimes it can be a difficult balancing act. To feel sad at the slipping of standards, but full of good cheer and harmony to all."

"Yes," said Bahir, "but the spiritual life has never been easy or black and white. The Master told us: concentrate on your own spiritual life, don't look around observing what others are doing or not doing. And can we really know who is close to the Master and who isn't? Perhaps slipping standards is the act of seeing slipping standards in others?"

"That sounds like a real Zen koan," said Alex.

"Yes, and don't forget the Master would offer such encouragement to disciples – even if from one perspective they were not following his highest spiritual path," said Bahir.

"Great, I like this" said Alex. "Now can I go and get a camera and record your philosophy on film for posterity?"

"Good man, Alex," said Bahir. "But let's leave the live audience for another day!"

AT THE RESTAURANT

Alex, Bahir, Duncan and Samir went out for breakfast.

"So how is it going Duncan?" asked Bahir.

"I'm going to set up a new business – an ice cream parlour," said Duncan.

"That's a good idea," said Samir. "The only thing I know about business is to choose a business for which you have a passion and expertise."

"I've already got deals with the suppliers and a great location. It's going to be amazing," said Duncan with an infectious enthusiasm.

"It's a good idea to put the ice cream parlour so close to the Ashram," said Samir.

"Yes, it should help attract a few regular customers," said Duncan.

"I don't know how you find time," said Bahir. "Here you are starting a new business, and you are still putting up posters all around town for our lectures. I have been doing this for the past 50 years, but when I retire and you take over, suddenly I see them in places I never thought to ask."

Duncan smiled and said, "I just go in with confidence they will want to take. Who could refuse such a beautiful poster of our Master? Plus, I like talking to people about things, then after our marathon conversations they always seem to want to take."

"Yes," said Alex, "after our marathon conversations, I'd take a poster too!"

"Duncan's perseverance and willingness reminds me of a story from many years ago," said Bahir.

"The Master asked a boy to invite a local priest to speak publicly in favour of the Master. But the boy thought there was no way a local priest would be willing to speak in favour of a spiritual Master who came from a different religious tradition. So, he didn't ask, thinking the Master didn't understand the way local priests have to be in modern society. When the Master heard, he had a sad face. He said a good disciple should be willing to try – even if it ended in outer failure. Sometimes the Supreme wants to offer people the option to take a divine action – even if there is very little chance they will be willing to do it. Just because people may turn down the spiritual Master's invitation, there can be a deep significance to just asking and giving them that opportunity.

"Anyway, after receiving this 'blessing' from the Master, the boy did go back and invite the priest. This priest had known the Master for quite a few years and he admired the Master's sincerity and purity of purpose. In response, the priest said, 'Thank you for giving me this opportunity, I have been wanting to do something like this for a few months now.' So the priest was happy and the disciples were illumined. On hearing about how events unfolded, the Master allowed himself a little smile and said, 'See, I do sometimes have a little inner vision.'"

"That is a good story," said Samir. "There are many more like it too." Sometimes the Master would ask us to speak with influential people. This kind of thing did not come easily to me. I felt the Master was asking this task as much for our spiritual benefit as anything else. When you spoke with people about the Master's philosophy, how much it could strengthen your own faith in the spiritual life. Sometimes, people were unexpectedly receptive to the Master. But equally others who you thought might be sympathetic to his philosophy didn't want to know. We certainly had many interesting experiences. Once, I was inwardly complaining about how I found this kind of experience difficult. But, as the Master often had the knack of doing, he began talking – as if picking up on my inward complaints.

"The Master began talking about the Mahabharata and the heroic divine warriors of those days. The Master said we should seek to cultivate that spirit of a divine warrior. The battlefield is not the outer violence, but the inner challenge of overcoming our ego – fighting insecurity, jealousy and pride, while being strong in our cultivation of faith and the spiritual life. The Master once gave a wonderful talk to some of us. He said we should become like divine warriors – we will show our strength not through haughtiness or a feeling of supremacy, but we will show our strength through our humility, courtesy, politeness and patience."

Bahir replied, "So it is great inspiration, Donald, when you have the confidence to speak about the Master's philosophy everywhere – from the launderette to ice cream parlour.

"Also, I remember my old friend Jahangir once told me a story. Our Master asked Jahangir to list all the achievements of his Ashram, so he gave quite an impressive list – concerts, public meditations, races, published books – and as an afterthought, he mentioned the number of photos they had put up to advertise these events. But the Master interrupted and said, 'No. You shouldn't mention this as an after-thought. Putting up posters is a real manifestation in its own right. Some seekers will see and feel something in my picture. They might not even come, but to see the consciousness of a spiritual Master may touch something inside them.' Also, the Master said that just going into shops and speaking with people can be a real manifestation itself.

"Although, Donald, I think that means talking vaguely about the spiritual life – talking about some of your 'interesting' theories h doesn't count!"

"Ha, ha! There's nothing wacky about the impending economic doom of Western civilisation," said Donald, without a trace of irony. "Anyway, as you know, I only talk about God and the spiritual life."

"Very good," said Alex. "Well in that case, we shall have to nominate Donald for disciple of the year!"

"Yes. Seconded," said Bahir. "I never thought somebody would come along and do a much better job than me. But, at the same time, I'm grateful to see you young seekers do something new and unprecedented."

"Well, Bahir," said Samir, "you weren't exactly a human dynamo, but to stick at the spiritual life and postering for 50 years, is no mean achievement. There's a lot to be said for that persistence which never gives up."

"Slow and steady sometimes wins the race," said Alex.

"But Duncan, about your business, I have one serious concern," said Samir.

"What is it?" said Duncan with a grave expression, "I've already sorted out planning permission with local government, I have the money to invest."

"No. It's something much more serious than that," said Samir.

"What is it?" asked Donald.

"Well, I'm worried – what if the owner eats all the ice-cream and leaves nothing for the customers!" said Alex.

Everyone burst out laughing – especially Donald, who seemed quite proud his reputation as a voracious eater preceded him.

Samir added, "That's the one problem of the new ice cream enterprise. My target to keep the weight under control is going to be tested."

Alex asked, "Do you think it makes a difference keeping weight down for the spiritual life? Did our Master say anything about this?"

"Well, I'm the right person to speak about this," said Bahir, "I only need to look at ice cream and the pounds come piling on. How I wish, in my next incarnation, I can have one of those metabolisms that keeps your weight always low. Anyway, from one perspective, weight doesn't matter. There were some spiritual Masters who were – let us say – heavy. Even the Buddha put on weight towards the end of his lifetime. Then there was Swami Dayananda – who was notoriously fat, despite hardly eating any food. But for us lesser mortals, I think weight can have a subtle effect. The physical is important. If we carry excess weight, we are carrying more of a load –physically, mentally and psychically. Based on the few occasions when I was able to lose weight, you do feel a greater lightness and this definitely helps in your meditation. Also, one other thing that comes to the mind, the Master once said, 'For every pound you lose, you lose a pound of jealousy and insecurity.'"

"I wonder why the Buddha put on so much weight, when he advocated a middle-path?" asked Donald.

"It is a good question," said Bahir, "but it is the same for all realised spiritual Masters – they can gain so much energy through their meditation, they are literally drinking nectar and light, so even with very few calories they can put on weight. Our Master said doctors would not believe the paltry number of calories he would eat but still put on weight. Also, sometimes the Masters accept food to be polite and give disciples and well-wishers the opportunity for service, so they end up putting on weight easily. But at the same time, they can totally transcend their weight."

"So are you're saying my generous layers of insulation are a sign of my spiritual height or not?" asked Donald.

"In your case, the Master might say big physique and big heart go together. But if you lose a bit of weight, you might inwardly fly even higher," said Bahir.

"Well, I'm getting into the right business," said Donald, "I might try the ice cream diet – eat ice cream three times a day – I'm sure that will help me lose weight!"

"Well, let me know how it goes," said Samir. "If you can prove eating ice cream is good for losing weight, you could set up two businesses for the price of one – sell ice cream and diet books at the same time."

"Excellent," said Donald, "I'm sure it's as good as any other diet."

MUSICAL ARRANGEMENTS

"Donald, how did you first come across the Master's music?" asked Prabhir.

"It was during one of my first meditation lectures. After the talk and meditation, a few boys performed some of the Master's songs. To me it was something entirely new. It moved me in a way that I never expected. I liked the meditations we did in the class, but also I felt I was not very good at doing them. However, when the small group of boys performed the music of the Master, the music touched something deep within and brought tears to the eyes, but it was not tears of sadness. I remember it was just two or three performers, and before it started, I didn't expect much, but as soon as the music and singing started, I felt transported. It was quite a simple and humble offering, but it made the experience of meditation very solid."

"Yes," said Prabhir, "soulful music can touch our psychic being. The Master says meditation and music are interchangeable. I remember vividly sometimes performing for the Master when he was still in the body. I joined a group of boys in singing a few of his songs. I particularly remember the silence before and after the singing. I understood why the Master said singing groups should meditate before and after a performance to assimilate the experience."

"What do you think of the way disciples arrange and perform the Master's music in recent concerts?" asked Donald.

"Well, thinking and opinions are always over-rated in the spiritual life!" laughed Bahir. "I once tried to learn to play the tambourine, but after a few years, I gave it up as a lost cause – so who am I to speak on music? When I hear some big groups I'm not sure about the music, but I definitely feel inspiration from their enthusiasm and cheerfulness. If disciples travel the world and offer this cheerfulness, light and positive energy, is this not a real manifestation?

"Everybody judges music by different criteria," continued Bahir, "but personally, when I listen to music in the Ashram, I am mostly interested in whether it helps or hinders my meditation. Sometimes the disciple music takes me to a very soulful place – other times, less so. But this kind of thing is not necessarily advisable to share. In an orchestra, it wouldn't work if everyone wanted to play the drums, or if people only wanted to play the violin. An orchestra requires diversity. During the Master's time in the physical, we heard a real diversity of musical performances."

"Don't you think that when we perform to the public, we need to make it more interesting?" asked Donald. "If we stuck to only acapella singing, with no instruments, would it not be too austere?

"Yes," said Prabhir, "there is something very powerful, poignant and beautiful about singing the Master's songs without any addition or arrangement. But I agree, there is also value in musicians adding to the music according to their inner feeling."

"To what extent did the Master encourage arrangements of his music?" said Donald.

"Well, that is an interesting question," said Prabhir. "There were times when the Master specifically asked a few selected disciples to make arrangements of his music. Often it was for a particular occasion – such as a visit by a dignitary. On these occasions, the Master wanted to give the big shot a good experience and felt an arrangement could add to the occasion.

"Sometimes the Master appreciated these arrangements, other times he didn't. There was one occasion when the Master expressed his disappointment with the spiritual standard of the performers. With a heavy heart, the Master said that when we perform in arrangements, seriousness and soulfulness disappear, and invariably get replaced with a vital exuberance. He said the essence of his original song gets lost. The Master was adept at not always expressing his real opinion. He hinted that his real opinion, which he had kept to himself for many years, waiting for the right time to share it."

"I'm surprised the Master would not reveal what he really thinks." said Donald.

"If the Master always judged his disciples according to strict spiritual standards, how many disciples would remain in the Ashram?!" laughed Bahir. "It's not just music but all aspects of the spiritual life. When we accept the Master as our Guru, we make a promise: 'Thy will be done.' But this theoretical surrender is one thing – transforming human nature is another." Also, it is a mistake to think it is all about music.

"The Master knew that his disciples could get attached to their creations, and he would give a certain freedom to our artistic inclinations. The Master was a supreme juggler – weighing up many different pressures and expectations from his disciples. Just because he allowed one disciple to take a particular route, doesn't mean that we should assume the Master felt that was the ultimate spiritual goal – far from it. If some disciples were very musical, the Master may have given more latitude to their creative musical spirit – especially if the Master felt they needed that to remain happy on the path. Keeping a disciple on the path could often outweigh many other factors.

"To go back to that particular occasion," said Prabhir, "during the talk someone asked the Master if that means we should never make arrangements of his music. The Master replied: no. He in fact had asked for these particular arrangements. Only he hoped that in the future when performing his music, we would bring our soulfulness to the fore and perform with a real spiritual feeling."

"One thing I would add," said Bahir. "In another context, the Master said it can be better to have action than inaction. When concerts are offered around the world, they do give joy to the participants and audience. Sometimes, I feel that I would like the Master's music to be closer to the original spirit of the Master's melody and the Master's tune, but what have I offered in the musical world? If you feel things could be better, it is much more preferable to lead by example, and not just say what others should or should not be doing."

"Anyway, it is all very good," said Donald, "but now I am a little confused as I have now heard contradictory things – that the Master both wanted arrangements and didn't want arrangements. Which is true?!"

"Well both, of course!" said Prabhir. "One complication is that there are different kinds of arrangements. In one type, singers sing the same words and melody as composed by the Master. But in addition, instruments add their own chords and a backing track to the main melody. The Master's melody is there, but instruments give an added interpretation to the song. Some music groups do a really fantastic job in offering a new dimension to the Master's music. I am really grateful for these performances. When I am tired, I often like to meditate to these musical performances.

"Another type of arrangement is what we might call vocal arrangements. This is where some or all of the performers use the Master's words, but sing a different melody, like a four-part harmony or just a new melody entirely. The vocal arrangements take the music very far from the initial composition of the Master. If the Master's melody is not there, it becomes a different song – a different consciousness. As the Master said: in his melody, aspiration is there.

"Now, as you can probably guess there is no black and white answer. The Master allowed some of his very accomplished musicians to create these vocal arrangements for certain occasions. I'm not sure whether it is right to say the Master encouraged it – perhaps tolerance is a better word. Then on another occasion the Master said, 'No more vocal arrangements,' but you could say this was the example of a rule with exceptions. To some extent, you can tie yourself in knots trying to work out what the Master said and what the Master really wanted. At the same time, you can listen to different versions of the Master's music and feel which move your heart. But everyone has to feel this for themselves. You have to expect and allow for a wide range of music preferences.

"On a personal level, if you take one of the Master's sacred songs and change the melody, I don't feel inspired to join in. To me it creates too much inner friction. It's like taking a beautiful flower and injecting some chemical to change the colour to a dazzling blue. It's not that dyed flowers are a bad thing per se. They are fine in their own way – some people like them – it is just that I get much more joy from the original flower. Sometimes when you try to change something that is already very beautiful, the original purity and joy get lost in the process. Also, it's a mistake to think this is only about music. The fundamental thing about our spiritual path is that we have to decide whether we want to please the Master in his own way or whether we want to please ourselves in our way.

One short story, which is amusing and maybe illumining. Piar was walking with the Master in a hotel where the disciples were staying. The Master had asked one of his excellent musicians to make an arrangement of a particular song. As the Master and Piar were walking, the Ashram Choir could be heard practising this very complicated arrangement, when suddenly from another room could be heard different music – a simple ballad by a widely known pop group. The Master stopped and said, 'From where to where?' Piar assumed the Master was referring to the difference in the consciousness between his own music and that of the pop group, so he was surprised when the Master pointed to the pop music and added, 'Listen to that – how simple it is, how beautiful.' And then, with a little bit of a scornful face, he pointed to the Ashram choir, 'Now listen to that!' The Master left more unsaid. You can fill in the blanks for yourself. The Master was always full of surprises!"

"What about people who create their own music and perform in the Ashram?" asked Donald.

"Throughout history, devotees have often turned to music to express their sincere devotion. If disciples feel inspired to write music, this is wonderful. However, everything has its time and place. When we meditate in the Ashram, how do we decide which disciple composition to play? Everyone will have different tastes and preferences. Also, we are spoilt because the Master composed so many songs. We have such a wealth of musical compositions direct from the Master, how can anything else give the same joy and peace?

"When you go to a lecture, you want to hear from the professor, you don't usually want to be taught second-hand by his students. One day the students may become great teachers themselves, but when you go to the professor's class, you want to hear direct from the source. Otherwise, you will lack confidence in the ability of his students, who have not yet passed their final exams. Also, another thing worth bearing in mind is that generally the Master wanted disciples to perform in groups. The Master felt solo performances are more likely to bring our ego to the fore. As usual, there were exception –, the Master specifically asked one or two singers to sing solo because they had a particular talent, and perhaps the capacity to be in the spotlight without suffering from pride. But these were special cases; as a general rule the Master felt much greater value in participating in a group.

"Also," said Prabhir, "it's not just about the mechanics of arrangements. It's also about the sincerity of the individual. Take the example of Paul. He spent literally hours daily singing the Master's songs acapella in a soulful and beautifully simple way. Then the Master said one day: now Paul, go and have joy making arrangements – use whatever instruments, you want, but it should be loud, energetic and dynamic!

"So here the master was encouraging both sides to his music. Now, perhaps there are other disciples in the audience secretly thinking, 'Great, I always wanted to start a jazz group.' But the Master never asked them – perhaps because they would focus exclusively on arrangements and not the simpler aspect of his music. Of course, this is only my speculation.

"Also, sometimes there is music performed and I don't particularly feel an affinity with the nature of the arrangement, but at the same time I really like the musicians involved. So, because of my oneness with the disciples, I like it – or you could say I try to like it! If asked, I always say very nice things! Who am I to take away people's joy and inspiration? You have to be very careful about doing that. It is always best to verge on the side of appreciating people's creative offerings. On the one hand you may say it is insincere flattery, but I feel it is more subtle than that. My appreciation stems from a genuine sense of oneness with the aspiration and goodwill of my friends. This attitude certainly gives more joy than worrying about what percentage of the Master's melody is in the music. But equally, when it comes to which music groups I will spend time practising with, I will choose those which give the most joy.

"It reminds me that when the Master performed in concerts on different instruments, often he wasn't perfect from a strict musical perspective. There were wrong notes, the Master may even struggle to make a sound. But, the experience of the concert wasn't about that. It was the consciousness of the Master. If you saw an edited video of some performances, your critical mind may come to the fore. You may not understand the Master. But when you were there, you experienced things from a different standpoint. It was like the Master was almost forcing us to decide – do you want to be in the mind or the heart? When we are in the mind, we count the wrong notes. When we are in the heart, we feel our oneness with the Master's meditation. When we are in this space, we get joy from the spirit of the music, not its outer perfection or lack thereof.

"I'm not saying disciples should give concerts and play a few wrong notes. No. The opposite. In fact, the Master always encouraged us to practise more and become better performers. At times, the Master's attention to musical perfection was revealing. In this regard, we shouldn't try to imitate the Master; our aspiration should be to strive for perfection. But sometimes I feel it is a mistake to worry too much about what we feel the public would want to hear. If we modify the Master's music to make it what we think is more 'palatable', then we are doing a great disservice to the public and an even greater disservice to the Master.

"Our role is to offer something new to the world. What is the point in imitating the rest of the world? There are already a million jazz and rock groups. Does the world need more of the same? We should be pathfinders for a new kind of soulful music, spiritual music; something that hasn't been on earth before. The Master offered so much to the world, but of all his creations, his music is the most accessible because it goes straight to the heart. So, this is what inspires me in the music world – the direct, unfiltered offering of the Master's music.

"Can I ask, does soulful music equal slow and ethereal?" asked Donald.

"I'm really glad you asked this question," said Prabhir. "No! Sometimes disciples make a mistake when they think the slower they sing, the more soulful they become. Sometimes, I think it is the opposite! If you listen to the Master's recordings he often sang with a good tempo – even for the most soulful songs – and also what power he injected into some songs. Again, we can't necessarily imitate the Master's style. For example, female singers sing in their own way. The sound is naturally thinner than the male voice. Apart from exceptional cases, we can't force ourselves to be something we are not. Soulfulness comes from our love for the song, singing with a sense of self-offering – trying to blend in with others, not standing out or singing with affectation. It is a remarkable experience if you can really sing in true oneness with other members of a group. It gives an even deeper understanding of the power of the Master's songs.

"Also, I'll tell you a short story. A good friend admitted to the Master that when he sang the Master's most sacred song, sometimes he started thinking about mundane things and he felt embarrassed to be disrespecting the song. I admired his sincerity, as it sometimes happens to me, but I don't think I would want to admit it to the Master! Anyway, the Master replied, 'You can sing a little faster so you don't have time for the mind to wander off.' I wouldn't have expected that answer, but it was quite illumining.

"On the theme of male and female singers on our path," said Donald, "like many other spiritual paths, in the Ashram there is a certain separation in activities between men and women. But what about music groups. What did the Master say about this?

"Donald, you should be given a prize for asking all the really good, interesting questions! But let me ask you: what about your own experiences in different groups?"

"Well," said Donald, "my observation is that when I have joined just male singing groups everything is quite simple and relaxed. When I sing in mixed groups, there is a different feeling – sometimes the awareness of a hidden tension below the surface."

"Yes, and sometimes, it is not even below the surface!" said Prabhir. "But it is perceptive what you say. When we perform, we like to be appreciated. Who doesn't want to be appreciated? But in a mixed group, there is the added aspect of human nature that particularly likes to impress the opposite sex. This story is as old as Adam and Eve. Until you realise God, is anybody immune? Also, when we perform music, we develop a very close inner connection with the other members of the group. We do this on an inner level. Our hearts open and we develop a musical connection. The best groups have this musical chemistry and understanding. So, if we are in a mixed group, we open ourselves to creating this inner, subtle connection. This is why the Master generally did not want groups to be mixed. He did make exceptions, for example when whole countries or particular cities performed together. You can find the other odd exception too. But at other times, the Master could be very strict in not wanting mixed groups. As the years advance since the Master's passing, this particular teaching can easily fade away. It is human nature to sometimes be better at remembering exceptions than anything else. But who is going to say anything? I'm certainly not!"

"What do you think the Master's musical legacy will be?" asked Bahir.

"That's a big question, and in a way we don't have to worry.

The Master's songs will stand for himself, whatever the disciples do. His soulful and haunting melodies will be there for others to discover. But sometimes in world history there have been completely new movements in music coming to the fore. For so long, music has been dominated by exuberant, vital music. I won't say anything against it; I listen to some myself. But the Master has created music that comes from a different plane. It is the music of the soul, and already – so soon after his passing – you feel this new branch of music is becoming accepted. From these small beginnings, something very special will come.

THE MIND'S RIGIDITY

"Do you ever think of questions that you wished you had been able to ask the Master?" asked Alex.

"Yes," said Bahir. "Since the Master's physical passing, many questions have come to mind. Of course, the spiritual thing to say is that in my deep meditation I hear the Master's inner guidance and this solves all questions. But unfortunately my deep meditation is often not deep enough! From one perspective it is true that we can feel and hear the Master's inner guidance from the inner prayer and meditation, but there is a difference between getting an intuition and hearing from the Master directly. There was always a great force in the Master's reply. You can doubt your own intuition – in fact, it is probably a good thing to be aware your own intuition may not always be right. With the Master, it wasn't just the outer words, but the spiritual force that accompanied them. You could always have confidence in both the Master's reply and the Master's spiritual force. This is why reading the Master's writings is so powerful – the words and force are there.

"I remember on one occasion, I wasn't sure how to deal with a particular problem. I was reading the Master's writings, and a particular talk seemed to give the right inspiration and guidance for the issue I was facing. The outer details it did not deal with, but the inner attitude – it was all there. Everything is in the Master's writings. Also, your question reminds me of two things. Firstly, the Master was always asking for more questions, and he would sometimes say: there are many good questions that have never been asked. But at the same time, the Master also said there is only really one question we need to ask – 'Who are we?' If we know who we really are, then all other questions become redundant.

"What about you, Alex, is there any question you would have liked to ask the Master?"

"Yes," said Alex, "if we do the wrong thing, thinking we are doing the right thing, will we be told when we go to the other side?"

Bahir laughed, "That's an interesting question. But the one I am more interested in is will other people be told that there were doing the wrong thing!"

"Yes," said Alex, "man's eternal prayer: Forgiveness-Light for me. Justice-Light for others!"

Bahir smiled, "I once read a book by a person who claimed he had psychic abilities. This psychic claimed that he could see and commune with spirits who had passed over to the other side. He claimed that when an atheist died and passed to the other side, even though he was no longer in the body, his mind so strongly identified with a materialistic worldview. He still didn't believe in God or the soul – even in the spirit world! I don't know if true, but I found it amusing. I guess that after death we don't suddenly become illumined. Perhaps we see the reality we want to see. If we think our religion is the only true light, will we become suddenly illumined by death? The mind's rigidity can be a very powerful force."

"Yes," said Alex, "it reminds me of that joke about Heaven. A man who recently died is being shown around Heaven by St Paul. It is very beautiful and he is very happy. But he sees a big building with high walls and enclosed ceiling. The man asks St Paul: what is in there? 'Oh that is for the Jehovah Witnesses. They like to think they are the only people who get to Heaven.'"

"Yes!" said Bahir. "For that joke, you can substitute many different religious sects – any religion which claims to be the only true way to God," said Bahir.

Bahir continued, "Sri Aaravananda once said something interesting. He said that young souls could often make faster progress than old souls. Old souls have more experiences and can be more powerful, but over their incarnations, they develop habits and patterns of thought that become quite ingrained. But with young souls – by contrast – there is greater flexibility and willingness. It can be easier for the Guru to mould these young souls according to his vision of the spiritual life."

"That is very interesting," said Alex.

"Of course, it depends on aspiration," continued Bahir. "There are young souls who want to experience the world and have no interest in spirituality. And then there are old souls who may feel after 600 incarnations of desires and suffering, perhaps it's time to try a spiritual incarnation!

"As you know, our Master's path is not just about silent meditation. Sometimes, how much the Master would encourage us to regain our lost innocence, joy and childlike attitude to life. This is the perfect antidote to the mind's rigidity. Once a year, he would ask us to perform skits, plays and circus acts, which required practice, skill and teamwork. Every year it seemed the Master was disappointed with our standard and unwillingness – and every year he would cajole and encourage us to take part. Of course, when you actually did participate, it was tremendous fun and you were grateful to the Master for pushing you out of your comfort zone."

"You should tell this to the new disciples," said Alex. "It seems this aspect of the Master's path is somewhat forgotten."

"Yes," said Bahir, "I remember the Master was once talking after our circus. He was saddened so many people did not want to participate. The Master said that when he was young his Guru insisted he get up at 3am and meditate for 8 hours a day – so by comparison he felt his request was relatively easy! Here our Master was asking us to participate in a simple act for five minutes and perhaps practise a few times. But the mind can resist because it involves breaking our comfortable habits and routines."

"Do you have more stories about the mind's rigidity?" asked Alex.

"Well, one anecdote I remember," said Bahir. "Once the Master gently waved his hand in the air and he said, 'Look at how the air moves with my hand – there is no resistance. The air is perfectly flexible.' The Master said flexibility was an important quality, because flexibility means we are willing to follow the Master's vision of the spiritual life. Quite a few times the Master would remember the story of Krishna and Arjuna. Krishna held up a fruit and asked Arjuna, 'What colour is it?' Arjuna replied, 'It is green.' And Krishna replied, 'No, it is blue. I see this as blue.' Now, Arjuna was fully surrendered to his Master. If his Master saw the fruit as blue, out of oneness, he would literally see the same colour as his Master. Arjuna would say, 'Yes, you're right, I can see the fruit is blue!'"

Alex asked, "Do you think Arjuna just said the fruit is blue or do you think he was actually able to see the ball as blue?'

Bahir replied, "That is an interesting question. From what I remember, the Master said Arjuna was able to see reality the way Krishna saw it. If Krishna said the fruit is blue – with his physical eyes – this is what Arjuna would see."

"Do you think that this illumining story can have relevance for our own spiritual life?" asked Alex.

"Yes. The story is important for any seeker. Suppose the Master says: I want you to perform in a circus act. Then at that particular time, the most important thing for our spiritual life is to perform in a circus act. However, the problem comes if we don't see it from the perspective of the Master. We think, 'No, perhaps I will enjoy sitting in meditation more.' Now, meditation is the bedrock of our spiritual life, but everything has its place. If the Master asks us to sing, and we think, 'No, I prefer to meditate in silence,' then we are following the spiritual life according to our own wisdom. If the Master asks us to sing, then at that time, we should take singing as our highest meditation. Once the Master said to us, 'For now, see spreading my light as your highest priority. See if you can grow our Ashram; your God-realisation can wait.' So, there our Master is asking us to place something higher than our own personal liberation."

"But, at the same time," said Alex, "if we follow the Master implicitly, is this not the fastest way to expedite our personal realisation?"

"Yes, I agree," said Bahir, "but the attitude is important. If we serve the Master expecting realisation in return, this approach is a mistake. We must serve the Master out of love and devotion, and feel that if the Master wants to grant liberation, we will be happy; if the Master doesn't want to grant liberation, we will also be happy."

"I had a good friend, Samar," continued Bahir. "Sometimes, the Master would ask Samar to do personal tasks for the Master, such as bring drinks, drive the Master or go out and buy food. I was full of admiration for how Samar would offer personal service to the Master for so many years. But if you are serving the Master day in and day out, year after year, this willingness and readiness are not always so easy to maintain. Once the Master rang up Samar and asked him to come to his house, and Samar replied, 'Sorry, I can't come just at the moment, I am in the middle of cleaning my house.' The Master replied, 'Fine,' and put the phone down. Samar said he was so absorbed in cleaning his house he wanted to finish before he lost the inspiration. After a couple of hours cleaning, he was very happy to have an immaculately clean house. He rang up another attendant of the Master and said he was free now. The Master's attendant said he would let the Master know.

"However, for several weeks, the Master never rang Samar at all. The invitations to serve the Master dried up completely. Samar had a lovely clean house, but he really missed the opportunities to serve his Master. It made him realise how much he valued those precious opportunities. Samar felt the Master was teaching him a lesson. True, the Master wanted us to keep our house very clean. But if the Master called you to do a service, that was the most important thing – the real service is to put the Master's needs before our own. We can finish off cleaning our house after serving the Master."

"On the one hand, it seems easy to criticise Samar," said Alex, "but I can imagine if I was in his position, there would be times when I might put my personal desires above serving the Master. For example, after this I am planning to go for a run; I really love running. But if someone rang up and said they needed some emergency help in the Ashram kitchens, would I have the surrender to forsake my run?"

"Yes," said Bahir, "of course, you could say getting a request from the head chef of the kitchens is not quite the same as getting a direct request from the Master in the physical! But if we are sincere, we will feel what the Master values and what the Master wants us to do. The important thing is that Arjuna's surrender was cheerful. He didn't say the fruit was blue because he wanted to just appear to say the right thing. His whole being was getting joy from seeing the world in the same way as his Master saw it. If we feel the Master wants us to serve in the kitchens, we should feel a sense of inner joy from doing this."

"But sometimes we have to do our duty, even if it may not seem as enjoyable," said Alex.

"Yes," said Bahir, "to feel an inner joy, whatever we do, is a very rarefied spiritual state. If we wait to get inner joy all the time, we may never budge an inch! Sometimes, I took on responsibility because I felt it was the right thing to do. At the time, it was anything but joyful. It needed doing and that was enough. But if you try avoid this responsibility, your conscience bugs you until it is done," said Bahir.

STORIES FROM THE SPIRITUAL LIFE, PART 2

IS THE FRUIT REALLY BLUE?

Alex said, "I've been thinking about the story of Krishna and Arjuna – I'm wondering whether new seekers would understand the story?"

Bahir replied, "To someone who has never meditated, the story may appear to make no sense. But when you start to meditate you realise there are different ways of looking at the world. In one state of consciousness the world can appear dull and boring. But spiritual Masters say, 'No. The world is a living miracle. Inside the tiniest flower, you can get so much joy – as long as you open your heart and take the time to appreciate.' Alex, you're a poet, can you remember the words of William Blake?"

Alex recited:

> "To see a world in a grain of sand
> And a Heaven in a wild flower
> Hold Infinity in the palm of your hand
> And Eternity in an hour"

Bahir continued, "William Blake was not a spiritual Master, he was a Seer-Poet. But these words have such mantric power. The question is – when we see a grain of sand, do we see an insignificant speck, or do we see the seed of infinity?

"Now, I never remember our Master saying a green apple is blue or anything like that. But on rare occasions, he did say that he saw in his disciples the living presence of God. Now, when we think of ourselves, we think of our doubt, insecurity, impurity and all that – the living presence of God we don't feel. But the Master is seeing the soul – our true nature, beyond the earthly form. The Master wants us to have faith in our inner divinity, but at the moment we don't see that in ourselves."

Alex asked, "Why do you think Krishna used the example of blue fruit for Arjuna?"

"I wish Krishna was here to answer!" said Bahir. "But my understanding is that Arjuna really wanted to be an unconditionally surrendered disciple; this is what Arjuna told Krishna. By saying the fruit was blue, Krishna was giving his dearest disciple the opportunity to actually live up to his promise."

"Yes," said Alex, "to talk of surrender is one thing. To actually implement is another."

Bahir continued, "Our Master once said that he did not have even one unconditionally surrendered disciple. Compared to great seekers of the hoary past, we are relative beginners, so it is more difficult to see things from a loftier viewpoint."

Alex said, "I was reading a book by Swami Adiyananda. He said that in deep meditation the world can appear as streams of light. Physical objects lose their sense of definition and separation – instead we see everything as a manifestation of light."

"Yes," said Bahir, "that is true and I do know some disciples who have had that experience. Also, quite a few disciples see the most beautiful aura around the Master. This shows that if two people go to see a spiritual Master they can experience different realities. Which is correct? A scientific materialist will say his way is correct; a seeker will say something else."

"It is like when I make dinner for the Ashram," said Alex. "Good disciples say, 'Thank you for the nutritious food.' Truthful disciples say, 'Oh Alex, I wish I'd gone out for pizza instead!'"

"Yes, both viewpoints are correct at the same time!" said Bahir.

"In Krishna's case, he knew Arjuna had the spiritual development to see beyond the outer form. After all, on the battlefield of Kurukshetra, Krishna had shown Arjuna his Universal, Transcendental Form.

"If you can see the Transcendental consciousness in your Master, you can see reality the way he sees it," said Bahir.

"Do you ever think it works the other way around? Do you think the spiritual Masters have to adapt to how their disciples see the world?" asked Alex.

"That is an interesting question," said Bahir. "Once, our Master was talking and he said something like, 'Suppose a mother was teaching her young child how to pronounce a word – like 'Massachusetts'. But her child insisted on mispronouncing it as 'Mass of shoes'. Eventually the Mother may give up on correct pronunciation and, out of love, she will start pronouncing the word the way her child does. She does this because she feels at that particular time, the child needs encouragement and joy rather than constant correction.'

"When the Master comes down from his highest meditation, he has the vision of creating Heaven on earth. The Master wants his spiritual children to aspire for this. However, maybe his spiritual children struggle to see and feel the same possibility as the Master. Out of necessity, the Master has to surrender part of his vision to earthly realities. Sometimes the Master gives up correcting his disciples because otherwise they will feel they are hopeless cases and perhaps even give up the spiritual life altogether. We need encouragement as well as correction. That is why the Master did not spend all day in samadhi – he lived and breathed a normal life, to show that we can also live this spiritual life."

"Can you think of examples of how the Master surrendered to the disciples in our own Ashram?" asked Alex.

"Maybe" said Bahir, "only I don't feel in the mood to think of examples just now. Today I prefer to marvel at how the Master has given so many seekers the opportunity to live a real spiritual life in the hustle and bustle of modern life – what is that if not a real miracle?

"It is true the Ashram is far from the highest vision of our Master, but perhaps that is the way it has to be at this stage in the world's evolution. We are all relative beginners – you can't get your PhD after one or two years of studying. Plus,

I'm sure we will have many, many incarnations in the future, where we will have the opportunity to transcend our current standard.

"Anyway, Alex, enough of philosophy. Do you fancy going out for pizza, or eating the leftovers from your cooking last night?"

"Let's go out for pizza!" said Alex.

"Excellent choice!" said Bahir.

UNCONDITIONAL FORGIVENESS

"The spiritual life is tough," said Donald with a long face. "It feels like I am always struggling to do what you are supposed to do."

"That might well be a very good sign," said Bahir. "The only real problem is when you think the spiritual life is easy, and that the spiritual life means just doing whatever you feel like doing. Don't feel bad if you sometimes fall short. Our religious culture in the past has often emphasised the concepts of sin and guilt, and it is hard to shake this off, even subconsciously. But the Master presents the spiritual life from a very different perspective. The Master says we are merely trying to grow from a limited light to a more illumined perspective. Guilt is a hindrance, but so is complacency. We came to the spiritual life precisely because we have so many weaknesses, and to transform this takes time. Be kind to yourself, but keep trying."

"How did the Master respond to people who fell short in the spiritual life?" asked Donald.

"Well, let's invite old Chetan over. He's the best person to speak on the subject!" said Bahir.

"Hey, Chetan, could you join us and share a story of how the Master reacted to those who fell short in the spiritual life?"

"Very good," said Chetan. "You mean I'm the right person to talk on the subject, eh?"

"Yes. It is one of your many capacities and talents," said Bahir.

"Well, as you know," said Chetan, "the Master could be very strict – especially with those of us who were physically close to the Master. Sometimes when you worked very hard for the Master, you felt like you deserved a little relaxation. If you do 99 good things for the Master, perhaps you feel you can start to follow your own sweet will for at least one or two things! I don't know why, but once old John decided to buy a few beers. Well, when the Master eventually found out, we all got scolded. The Master made it clear that we shouldn't turn a blind eye if our fellow monks were doing something wrong. It was like we were all connected – a spiritual band of brothers, if you like.

"If one of us did something great, it was the success of the whole group, but when one monk did something wrong, it was also our whole responsibility. I don't think it was the small quantity of alcohol affecting John's meditation that displeased the Master, but the disobedience. The Master gave a talk in which he said the outer obedience is so much easier than the inner obedience, and if we can't follow basic rules, we are never going to progress in the spiritual life.

"Anyway, a few weeks later, this experience is still in the back of our minds. We were at the Master's house when the Master received news about a dear disciple called Graham. Graham was very close to the Master, if a little wayward and unpredictable. Despite this, the Master frequently showered his affection, concern and love on his beloved disciple – even if sometimes we wondered at the mystery of why and how the Master would praise and scold different people. Alas, on this occasion, Graham's unpredictable nature had landed him in trouble. He had ended up going to a bar and getting drunk. Very nicely he had ended up in a police cell for causing a disturbance!

"So, we were sitting there secretly thinking that this time Graham had really gone too far, and surely the Master's elastic would snap. But the Master didn't react as we thought he might. The Master said with infinite sweetness and concern, 'O my Graham.' The Master's eyes expressed such love, compassion and forgiveness. There was no word of judgement to say nothing of condemnation – only divine concern. The Master only wanted us to go and bail Graham out of jail and make sure he was looked after and well fed."

"That is a great story, but why did the Master react so differently to a more serious issue?" said Donald.

"Who can fully understand the ways of the Master?" said Chetan. "But on that evening we had a glimpse into a particular aspect of the Master – the Master's aspect of unconditional love and forgiveness. It says in the Master's writings that wherever we go – even if we go to the lowest hell – the Master will follow there with us. But do we really believe this? We judge the Master with our human mind. Because our mind is always judging, we assume the Master will be judging from our same standard. But the Master's realisation is far beyond this. In the soul's world, judgement slips away and there is only unconditional love. This is a true story.

Once I was with the Master and he meditated briefly, but with incredible intensity. For some reason, the Master enabled some unusual receptivity, and at the Master's glance, I had an experience of this wave of unconditional love flooding my whole being. It was an ecstatic feeling. It only lasted a few minutes, but who can forget that experience?"

"If the Master is beyond judgement," said Donald, "how come the Master is so strict and judgemental at seemingly small infractions?"

"Well, this is the wonderful paradox. As the Master said, 'Do you want my forgiveness or my compassion?' If you want only my forgiveness, you can do whatever you want and my unconditional love will be there. But, if you want more light, if you want transformation, then you have to follow the spiritual discipline and the spiritual path. We don't come to the Master's path just to receive the Master's forgiveness. We come because our soul wants to transform our nature. This is the Master's job – scolding his disciples, in the hope they will make progress. What is hard to believe is that at the same time as our Master scolds us, he is still offering his unconditional love."

***

"This conversation reminds me of something," said Bahir. "I was talking with Virhat many years ago. He was a very good disciple – quiet and undemonstrative, the kind of disciple who did a lot of work that most people were unaware of. Anyway, he said that when he was a newish disciple, he was full of aspiration and eagerness to please the Master. He would hear the Master scold other disciples, and inwardly he had this feeling that he would never do these things or displease his Master. He had this what you might call confidence. But then, unexpectedly, he got scolded by the Master. He was involved in something which he managed to justify to himself. But when the Master found out, he was warned that if he did it again, he would have to leave the Ashram.

"It was quite a defining moment. He realised his previous self-congratulation was misplaced – he wasn't doing as well as he believed. But he took the Master's scolding as a real double blessing. Firstly, it helped him to overcome a particular difficulty in his spiritual life, and secondly, it really helped him to cultivate humility and reduce his false spiritual pride. This humility was evident in his life, and you realise what a strong foundation it can make. It also taught him to be less judgemental – just because disciples have some difficulty or weakness, almost inevitably we all have some different difficulty.

"After hearing his story, I started complaining to Graham about some things going on in the Ashram and he patiently listened. But then he said, 'Yes, some people can easily forget things. For example, prasad is prepared ready to be taken at the end of a function. And prasad is a very sacred moment to the Master. But the problem is that when it is left out, some take early and enjoy a snack, sitting outside eating whilst the function is going on.' Now the interesting thing is I was 'caught', because the previous night I had done that same thing myself! I'd had a hard day – I was cold, tired and hungry and felt like some food. So, I took prasad – there's no one to tell you not to these days – and I sat outside eating and chatting with friends. Now the interesting thing is that when doing this, I was aware of a faint sense of doing the wrong thing, but it was easy to override this inner voice because I felt I deserved it after serving the Master all day. When Graham mentioned this issue indirectly, I felt like I saw everything very clearly. With prasad you have to take it in the Master's way or it ceases to be prasad and becomes even disrespectful.

"It was a humbling experience – it is so easy to see what others are doing wrong, but so easy to think you cannot do anything wrong yourself! As I have said before, the human mind has tremendous capacity for self-justification.'

"Also, with Graham's story of getting caught, it reminds me that sometimes disciples would actually say to the Master, 'Master, if we do the wrong thing one time out of a hundred, that one time always seems to be the moment when you appear to catch us in the act. When we do the right thing, we never see you. But, if one second we slip, then as if by magic, you seem to appear out of nowhere!'

"The Master smiled and said, ' Yes. See, I am doing my job! If you are doing the right thing, you are helping me and my mission and I can concentrate on other things. But if your standards slip, is it not my job to put you on the right track?' Many disciples reported that experience."

Donald piped up, "So should I go around telling disciples what they are doing wrong?"

"Yes! You can tell Bahir what he is doing wrong every day!" said Chetan, "I think that will help him to make tremendous progress! But, more seriously, I would actually advise doing the exact opposite. If your fellow monks do 99 wrong things and one good thing, try to catch them when they are doing a good thing and make a point of appreciating it."

"Sounds like good advice!" said Donald.

STORIES FROM THE SPIRITUAL LIFE, PART 2

DETACHMENT, INNER AND OUTER

Donald asked Bahir, "Could you speak about why the Master wished his male and female disciples to avoid mixing?"

Donald replied, "Well, there is a well-known story about detachment that I would like to share.

***

"Two monks are out walking when they see a young woman getting into difficulty while trying to cross a turbulent river. The elder monk, Kosai, stops for a moment and then decides to help the woman get to the other side. The crossing happens without incident, and after reaching the other side, the woman expresses her gratitude to Kosai. Kosai modestly responds by offering a short bow and brief smile before they return on their journey.

"The younger monk, Shunkan, says nothing, but inwardly he is thinking about how Kosai is breaking the monastic rules that monks should not touch women. After a few hours of walking, the two monks return to their monastery. After an evening meal and meditation, they are sitting informally with their spiritual teacher, Dosho. Dosho leans back in his chair and, as if sensing something is amiss, asks his two disciples about their journey. The younger monk, Shunkan, is silent for a moment, and then states, 'Well, the thing is, I have to report that Kosai broke the monastic rules in carrying a woman across the river.'

"Dosho closed his eyes and was silent for a moment. Then he briefly smiled and replied, 'In this case, I can see that Kosai carried the woman across the river, but after carrying her across, he put it out of his mind. He left her at the river. However, in your case, you have been carrying the image of the woman around in your mind ever since. So Kosai has developed a degree of detachment.'

"Dosho continued, 'Monastic rules are there for a very good reason and not an unyielding religious dogmatism. Of course, if we are insincere, it is easy to find convenient reasons to break rules. If we are sincere, we will happily follow them. However, in this case, Kosai went deep within and felt that this was a unique circumstance – helping protect human life is more important than the rigid adherence to monastic rules. So Kosai prayed for protection and saw himself as an instrument. When he had finished carrying the woman across, he let go of the incident from his mind. Outwardly he was touching the woman, but inwardly, he was praying for detachment.'

"'Of course, always we have to try to follow the monastic rules – real exceptions will be very rare. But more important than the outer adherence is the inner detachment. We may never speak to women, but if our mind is always thinking about impressing our girlfriends and what others are thinking, we have to know our outer monastic vows are worthless. We would be better returning to the ordinary life of emotional entanglements.'

"Dosho was silent and then added, 'Dear Shunkan, don't be

hard on yourself. You are a good monk. Just focus on the spiritual life and your own meditation, and you will find you are slowly and steadily able to transcend these old vital thoughts. The detachment Kosai has, you too can gain over time.'

"Now that story I have told with my own embellishments," said Bahir, "but the interesting thing is – what happens next? I'd like to suggest three different possibilities from my own imagination.

***

"In the first possibility, Kosai, the older monk, becomes secretly rather proud of his detachment. Over the next few weeks, he starts to feel he is capable of always maintaining the highest spiritual detachment. When female visitors come to the monastery, he starts spending time chatting to them and acting as spiritual counsellor. He feels he has gone beyond human attachments and is perfectly safe. But, alas, after a few months, he finds he has fallen in love! All his peace of mind has gone, and instead he finds himself in a whirlwind of emotional turmoil. In his meditation, all he can do is think about his new girlfriend and the stress of trying to keep it quiet from the other monks in the monastery.

"Now, after a few weeks of this inner turmoil, his Guru, Dosho, calls all the monks together and relates to them a story.

"'Many years ago,' begins Dosho, "there was a very advanced seeker called Tensai. Tensai would meditate for 8-10 hours a day, and this was not just sitting quietly but a very deep meditation with a real renunciation. Tensai's Guru rarely saw him outwardly, but inwardly he was keeping a very close eye, as he knew Tensai had the capacity to attain enlightenment in this incarnation.

"'Now, Tensai was meditating in a secluded temple, just outside the main monastery, but because he was so absorbed in meditation, he would often forget to get any food. One day, a beautiful young woman came to this temple and was deeply impressed with the beauty and spiritual countenance of Tensai, she said to Tensai, 'I would dearly like to bring you food and help you in your spiritual journey.' Now, Tensai had very rarely had any interaction with women during his intense sadhana of the past few years, and at first he wondered if it was the right thing to do. But then he remembered the story of the emaciated Buddha being given rice milk by Sujata. It was this rice milk that taught the Buddha the importance of a middle path and ultimately helped Siddhartha to become enlightened.

"'So Tensai took it as an auspicious sign and gratefully accepted. Every day, this beautiful woman came to visit Tensai to offer food and sustenance. As the days went by, she began asking more questions, and they talked about subjects related to the spiritual life. These conversations become more frequent and long-lasting, and Tensai started to think more about these meetings, cutting short his meditations because he had different thoughts going around in his head.

"'But then, one day out of the blue, Tensai's spiritual Master came bursting into the temple. Tensai's Guru was real old-school Zen! He started shouting and berating this poor woman. Tensai's gentle nature was shocked by his Master's fierce language. After the woman ran away, Tensai's Guru looked at Tensai and said, 'What are you doing? You are on the verge of realisation and here you are getting involved with a beautiful woman. Don't you listen to anything I say?! She talks of spirituality, but I can inwardly see that her spirituality is also mixed with more worldly ambitions. You think I am being rude? Well, I don't care what society thinks! My only divine mission is to lead my disciples to realisation. I will insult everyone in town if it keeps my disciples on the right path!'

"'Tensai's initial shock dissipated and he realised that deep down his Guru was right. He went back to focusing on his meditation and ultimately he did achieve enlightenment.

"As Dosho finished the story, he looked very serious and slowly walked back to his quarters.

"Now, after hearing this story from his Master, Kosai was cut to the core. He knew he could not keep anything from his Master on the inner level. The next day he sought out his Master and, with tears in his eyes, said, 'Master I have fallen so much. I have become entangled!'

"Dosho looked up at his dear disciple and said, 'Do you think this is news to me? Inwardly I always know when my disciples are in trouble, but sometimes I have to let things play out in the outer world. Now, Tensai, you need to stop all this emotional nonsense and get back on track right away. Do you think your soul brought you to me just so you could enjoy a romantic fling? The best thing is for you to immediately leave the monastery and go on a pilgrimage to Mount Kenzo. Come back in a few months and all this will be forgotten, but never become proud of your detachment and spiritual height again!'

"Tensai was so grateful for the wisdom, love and forgiveness of his Master, and immediately set out for Mount Kenzo, chanting the Buddhist mantras all the way.

***

"So, that was the first possibility, Donald!" said Bahir.

"Wow, that's a great story!" said Donald. "Do you think our Master would react like the Guru of Tensai?"

Bahir laughed, "Well, our Master was not 'old-school Zen'. He would never scold someone from outside the Ashram, though he might scold the disciples! But the principle of protecting his disciples from romantic entanglements was exactly the same – even if it meant his own manifestation suffered."

"Anyway, the second story is a little shorter," continued Bahir,."In this version of 'What happens next?' Kosai remains truly detached from the life of girlfriends and lower-vital pleasure. But he is still very proud of his detachment. Therefore, he feels he can start enjoying the company of women visitors to the Ashram. It is mostly innocent and Kosai is able to maintain his inner detachment. As soon as he enters into meditation, the past disappears from his mind and he experiences a deep inner peace. However, although he is friendly with women visitors in a purely innocent way, the younger monk Shunkan starts to feel jealous of Kosai. Shunkan imagines that these relationships are much deeper than they actually are.

"Shunkan is trying to follow the monastic way of life, but he becomes deeply jealous of the fact that he can't have both the detachment of Kosai and the company of young women. Shunkan is tempted to leave the monastery out of frustration. However, fortunately, an old monk, Huang, is observing the situation and speaks very compassionately to the young Shunkan. Kosai says, 'Jealousy is a very powerful force both for making us unhappy and also – like anger – causing us to see things that are not really there. Let us try to see jealousy as a reminder that we need to work on our inner transformation. When jealousy is making us miserable, it shows us that something isn't quite right, but remember it doesn't have to be like that.' Shunkan is grateful for this advice, and he realises how much negative energy he had spent thinking about Kosai and blaming Kosai for his own weaknesses. Instead of leaving, Shunkan works hard to overcome his jealousy. At the same time, Kosai also becomes aware of the effect he is having on Shunkan, and so feels the inner necessity to set a better example and be more thoughtful of his younger brothers.

***

"In the third possibility, Kosai remains deeply humble – despite his Master's outer praise. He knows his detachment was only due to the grace of his Master, and he should never take anything for granted. When welcoming visitors to the monastery, he is always careful to remain a respectful distance from female visitors. He is unfailingly polite and kind, but wearing the ochre robes of spiritual detachment, he feels he is standing as a symbol for those who aspire to follow the spiritual life.

"In this version of the story, Shunkan is deeply impressed by the humility, modesty and purity of his elder brother disciple and is inspired to throw himself more wholeheartedly into the spiritual life. He finds that by associating with older monks, over time, he makes real progress in becoming detached from his past thought patterns and emotional vital tendencies. As the years go by, Shunkan realises that the rules become insignificant – the rules are no longer there as something to jump over, but the spiritual life of purity is something that is coming spontaneously, without pressure or tension.

Shunkan never forgets the incident of Kosai carrying the woman over the river. But rather than remembering with jealousy or frustration, he remembers it as an inspiring example of how we can aspire to complete detachment and – as long as we remain humble and careful – how we can slowly transform the frustration and limitation of human love into the all-embracing divine love."

***

"So which character do you identify with?" asked Donald.

Bahir laughed, "I will only say that I quite like the story of Socrates visiting the Oracle of Delphi."

Donald smiled, "Bahir, you do like to answer in riddles and stories!"

Bahir looked pleased with himself, "Yes, I suppose so!"

Donald said, "Well you had better tell me the story of Socrates visiting the Oracle of Delphi."

"OK," said Bahir. "Socrates went to the Oracle of Delphi with a few disciples. On arrival, the Oracle of Delphi looked at the palm of Socrates and started insulting him.

"The Oracle said, 'I can clearly see that Socrates has insecurity, pride, jealousy, impurity and doubt.'

"At this, the disciples of Socrates started to get mad and wanted to thrash the oracle. But Socrates said, 'No, wait. Let us see if she has anything more to say.'

"The Oracle continued, 'Yes. Although Socrates has all these negative qualities, he keeps them at an arm's distance – he has mostly detached from these qualities.'

"I like this story because unless we are one of the extremely rare God-realised souls, we all have these inner weaknesses, which are always lurking beneath the surface. Our job as spiritual seekers is to remain humble and alert, and always try to recognise them when they appear. Sometimes, I see jealous thoughts arise – almost innocuously – but when they come, I say, 'Jealousy, I hate you, it is beneath my dignity to indulge in you.'

"I'm not saying I've conquered jealousy, impurity and all that – no, they always lurk there. But I try to create the circumstances where they don't arise as much, and then I try to be aware and reject them as soon as they make an appearance. Sometimes I'm more successful than other times, but as long as we keep trying to transform our nature what else can we do? The only failure is when we just surrender to these negative forces."

THE SECRET TEACHING

Bahir and Duncan were seated in a quiet coffee shop.

"So, Bahir, did the Master ever give any secret teaching to a select few disciples?"

"Oh yes, I believe so!" said Bahir.

"So, what was it, Bahir?" asked Duncan.

"Well, nobody told me! Let me tell you a short story though," continued Bahir. "I've always struggled with high blood pressure. Never paid too much attention, but my mother used to worry on my behalf. One birthday, she is all excited and says she has found a 'secret' esoteric cure for high blood pressure. (It cost $500 so was definitely a limited edition). So, I open up this box holding the elixir of good health. There are all these ornaments and trinkets – crystals, 'special' incense and a cassette of music. To me they are nothing, but the main tool is a 'meditation exercise'. This sparks my interest a little, so I read the instructions and it involves very rhythmic breathing through alternative nostrils. It sounds quite interesting, but also gives a sense of familiarity. Anyway, I practise the exercise and feel it has a benefit. But a few days later, I'm reading the Master's book and I remember why it is familiar. The exercise is almost word for word, the same as the Master's – except the term God has been substituted for something more secular!

"So, this secret elixir of good health had actually been freely available in the Master's writings for a few decades!"

"So did the exercise work for reducing blood pressure?" asked Duncan.

"I'm not sure really. But it is a very good meditation exercise for quietening the thoughts. Since it cost so much, I told my mother it worked!"

"People give more value if you have to pay," said Duncan.

"There is something in that," said Bahir. "But going back to the secret teachings. In the past, there were esoteric societies who did keep a degree of secrecy. This was often for their own protection. In the past, mystical practices were often misunderstood and minority groups could be persecuted. Also, perhaps there was a time when spiritual Masters felt the general population were not ready for a real spiritual life and deep meditation. But our Master's path is very accessible for anyone with sincerity. More than anything, the Master sought to show spirituality is something very natural, normal and everyone's birthright. Even if people don't feel ready for all the Master's teachings, there is something for everyone."

"That's all very good, but I was kind of hoping for a special meditation technique?" asked Duncan.

"In the very early days, the Master had a new disciple and after a few weeks, this new disciple asked for a special meditation. So, the Master gave him a very specific exercise. A week later, this new disciple said the meditation wasn't working and could he have another one. The Master obliged and gave him an individual mantra. But, a week later, the same story – the new disciple was complaining the exercise wasn't working. This time, the Master didn't give a new exercise, but asked, 'How often do you practise these exercises?' The new seeker said, 'Once or twice a week.' So after that the Master rarely gave individual meditations – he felt it was unnecessary and not helpful."

"Yes, I know really." said Duncan. "Meditation isn't about technique, as Alex often says. But how do you get more aspiration and more soulfulness in meditation? There must be something I can do to accelerate my spiritual progress," said Duncan.

"This is a good question, and I'm not sure I'm the right person to answer about rapid spiritual progress. But it does make me remember the old days when I was a very new disciple. I went to visit the Master for the first time. I was very eager and couldn't wait. Other disciples had told me about their wonderful experiences with the Master, so I half-thought that all I had to do was turn up, meditate and Heaven would literally descend. The problem was that because I had so much expectation, it was a frustrating experience. Over the years, I learned to let go of expectation and develop more patience. The Master always said you couldn't push or pull spiritual progress. Now, Duncan, you already have sterling aspiration, but patience will strengthen and make it more solid. It's like baking bread – you've done the hard part of getting all the ingredients and putting them in the oven, but you then have to let the loaf rise of its own accord."

"If you take the loaf out too soon, you get indigestion!" said Duncan.

"Yes, and then you may end up throwing the half-baked bread away!" said Bahir.

"But there is one thing I can share which you may find of interest," said Bahir. "I once spoke to Bhagat, who spent many hours with the Master in person. Bhagat told me that the Master would go through periods of repeating japa many thousands of times. Now, after a spiritual Master has realised God, he doesn't need to meditate or practise spiritual discipline in the same way. But sometimes they continue to do spiritual disciple – both to inspire their disciples, and also perhaps to meditate on our own behalf. I often pondered about this, as the Master rarely talked about his japa – he just did it of his own volition.

"Anyway, once the Master suggested to Bhagat that he could try japa and build up to several thousand a day. Now, Bhagat never did – he was too busy serving the Master. But, since retirement, I have found the time to do japa and I really like it. I built up slowly but feel it helps bring a calmness to the mind and awakening to the heart."

"I've not heard this before," said Duncan.

"And probably for good reason," said Bahir. "I definitely heard a recording of the Master say on the radio that 'japa' is not necessary on our path. Our path is the path of the devotional heart. If there is an opportunity for service to our Mission, but I stay at home counting japa beads, I feel the Master would be very displeased. But, if you cut out time-wasting and make an effort to spend 10 minutes doing japa in the morning and at lunchtime, you can definitely get some benefit."

"That's great," said Duncan, "I will do 10,000 a day!"

Bahir gently laughed and said, "Well, I don't know, 500 a day would be a good start. With mantra – like many things in life – it can feel that at first you have to work really hard to make any progress. But, if you persevere, you start to gain momentum and then it feels easier and more natural to continue. The Master used the analogy of turning a big, heavy wheel. At the start, you have to make so much effort, and the wheel barely moves. At this point, it's tempting to give up, but if you persevere and the wheel starts to move, then the wheel creates its own momentum – then you need less effort to keep the wheel spinning. With meditation and mantra, getting into that daily rhythm is the challenge. But also, Duncan, you already do so many good things – working on your business and postering. It is possible you will make more spiritual progress through doing these things as well as you can. I wouldn't sacrifice any of that for japa. I happen to like japa, but I'm an old man with time on my hands. It is not necessarily for everyone. It is a mistake we disciples can make – just because something is good for us, we think others should do it too – but, we all have different paths."

"Why do you think the Master said one thing on radio and something else to an old disciple?"

"Well, that is an interesting question," said Bahir. "Firstly, it is a very different audience. On radio the Master was talking to a public audience and perhaps wanted to stress the essentials of our spiritual path – love, devotion, the path of the heart. Maybe japa is something the Master feels will help those who are already well established in the spiritual life. Spirituality has certain building blocks – meditation, service, kindness, purity and a balanced approach. When we have this solid foundation, only then might it be appropriate to add on more advanced aspects."

"You mention balance. I was reading a book by Swami Adiyananda – he said next to an Ashram, you should always have a mental asylum too!"

"Well, yes, maybe!" said Bahir laughing. "Even spiritual Masters can have a dry sense of humour. But balance is certainly important. If we spend all day chanting, 'I am God,' this is the wrong approach. We need the spiritual life to be grounded in reality. That is why the Master was keen for his disciples to work, do sport and live a balanced life.

"Does that mean I should balance my deep meditation with going to the movies afterwards?"

"Well, perhaps not that kind of balance! If we have a lofty meditation, why go and lose it all watching a silly movie? There are better ways to relax and remain in good spirits."

"Like go with your friends to an ice-cream parlour?" said Duncan.

"Exactly, Duncan. Who needs japa when we can eat your spiritual ice cream? I'm sure there's something special in your unique varieties."

"Yes. You should work up to 10 scoops of ice cream a day. I assure you it will help you with your diet."

"Alright, Duncan, that's it. I'd like you to become my weight-loss Guru. I have implicit faith in your faith in ice cream!'"

AN AWKWARD CHARACTER

"How do you make a living, Daniel?" asked Bahir.

"I work at a local restaurant in town. It is quite hard work, but we are kept busy and so time passes quickly." Daniel replied.

"Do you like working there?" asked Bahir.

"Yes, I do quite like working there. When I first started working there, I saw it as just a job, but the owner inspired a different attitude because he was always trying to improve every aspect of the restaurant. He examined everything – from orders to service and organisation – to see how we could make it better. He never accepted the philosophy of 'good enough' – he wanted always to improve. He was a hard taskmaster because he was never content to accept a low standard. Literally, every day he came in and thought, 'What can we do to improve?' It meant you had to be on your toes, but at the same time, work became something to look forward to because you enjoyed the challenge and sense of purpose. He wanted us to create a better restaurant, but he realised that creating a better business relied on starting with a good harmonious feeling amongst the workers. Although he was trying to improve the standards of the business, it was done with an attitude of making us feel responsible for the success of the restaurant. If we had a good idea, we could make a suggestion and if he felt it was good, he was very willing to incorporate it. This sense of delegation and responsibility for our particular areas meant we all felt committed to the success of the restaurant, and this was far more important than the wage we received."

"You're lucky to have a boss like that," said Bahir. "It is rare to combine those two traits of aiming for a better business while also creating a positive atmosphere where the workers feel responsible for the success or otherwise of the business. Many years ago, I worked in a restaurant, but the boss had a dismissive attitude toward his workers. All he cared about was increasing profits. He would penny-pinch in cutting costs but was tremendously reluctant to give any appreciation to those who worked really hard. Instead, he would criticise us, despite the difficulties of working on a limited budget. It created a disharmonious feeling so I didn't stay long. All the best staff ended up leaving so the business wasn't profitable at all. People will work for low pay, but they won't work for both low pay and no appreciation."

"Yes," said Daniel, "but unfortunately the problem is that the boss has left to go and set up more restaurants overseas. He comes back occasionally but he has left responsibility of the restaurant to other supervisors. However, because there isn't the same strong leadership, there is greater confusion and mixed opinions about how to proceed."

"Sometimes, you just have to get on with your own job as best you can," said Bahir.

"True, but I often get worked up with one of the supervisors who is often undermining the old boss's approach to the restaurant. This supervisor, Henry, is a good chap, but in the restaurant, he's constantly trying to change the working methods that worked so well in the past. Now, people realise that if they slack off or come in late, Henry will say this is all fine and the boss wouldn't mind. If you try to counter and say our boss was a stickler for coming to work on time, Henry will manage to remember something different and it leaves you thinking, 'Am I remembering things correctly?' It always feels a little disconcerting when people remember something different to what the boss actually said about the restaurant."

Bahir replied, "Unfortunately, it is human nature to remember what we want to remember. Often we don't deliberately lie, but we can become selective with the truth, and if we are insincere we can remember whatever we want to justify our way of looking at the situation. This aspect of human nature is as old as Adam and Eve. It would be a mistake to feel Henry is the only person in the world with this trait!"

"Yes," said Daniel, "but it is a little frustrating, as sometimes I challenge Henry and say something like, 'Well, our boss didn't really mean that we could just please ourselves.' But then Henry seems to subtly enjoy the fact I'm worked up, and it encourages him to push the boat as far as he can. I do like Henry – he has many good qualities – but when he subtly undermines the effective structure that our boss set up, it makes me frustrated, because work is less fulfilling when you don't have that unity of purpose. You want to maintain the good reputation of the restaurant, but it is harder when the supervisor isn't as committed as our former boss."

"Well, it sounds like Henry is a bit of an awkward customer," said Bahir. "You should come and work in the Ashram enterprises – no awkward characters there. Only saints in the making – as you know very well!"

"Yes. Well, I like your definition of a saint! On that basis, I think even I might meet your criteria for a saint."

"Well, I don't know about that Daniel! But then if you keep visiting old Gopal to cheer him up, you'll definitely earn a few bonus points in the inner world," said Bahir.

Bahir continued, "Now, fortunately or unfortunately, it's got to that point in the day when I feel like sharing a bit of philosophy and you are the lucky or unlucky recipient!"

"Firstly, even if you were to leave the restaurant, you would almost certainly meet other people like Henry. Secondly, we can have a good heart but our mind and vital can sometimes get a little malicious, unconscious pleasure in creating a mini-drama. When Henry sees you are a little agitated because you confront his perception of the restaurant, it may encourage him to do it even more. Consciously he may not realise, but he may enjoy seeing you worked up! It's not necessarily just about wanting to change the restaurant, but also partly because he enjoys being the centre of attention.

"Sometimes the best way to treat someone like Henry is to outwardly smile and maintain a friendly approach. When he tries to goad you with things that you know are not right, don't get sucked into an argument. It will be mostly counter-productive. Also, though it may be tempting, if you spend your time criticising the way he is, you will just harm yourself. If we spend time criticising people doing the wrong thing, it affects our consciousness, and we get sucked into the same mindset. It is better to try and stick to your path and way of working. Where possible, just go straight ahead and focus on your work – don't try to change Henry's nature; that is not possible. Our Master said that when we criticise others it leaves an indelible stain on our own heart. If we spend our time criticising 'bad' people, we can easily become one of those 'bad' persons ourself. If we sling mud back, do we not get covered in mud too? We have to be careful. This is the time for us to truly try and be saints. Maintain goodwill to all. Don't feel responsible for the world, and don't forget it is only a restaurant. Your only real responsibility is your very own spiritual life. Whatever other people do, say or believe, you are 100% responsible only for your own spiritual progress and devotion to the Master. It is your former boss who has to maintain responsibility for his restaurant; for you, what really matters, is how you respond to the situation.

"It can be challenging when the Henrys of this world seem to undermine our efforts, but that's the way the world is. As our Master might say ,'It thickens the plot.' I think this wonderful phrase means that when we come up against challenging situations, it provides us with an opportunity to put into practice our spiritual philosophy. Anyone can read the Bhagavad Gita and admire the philosophy of equanimity and devotion to God – but can you implement it in the hustle and bustle of life? That is the real test. Also, don't focus on the negative – it sounds like you were very lucky to have a good boss, even if just for a few years, and as a result you've learnt a lot. Don't wait for perfection in your work situation, as it will never come. Just set a good example, and other workers in the restaurant will appreciate your hard work and adherence to your boss's standards.

"I told you I was in a philosophic mood, Daniel," said Bahir.

"Well, it's pretty helpful. And as you say, it's only my outer workplace," said Daniel.

Bahir continued, "Yes. It reminds me of a story. There was a boy in the Ashram who had many very divine qualities, but after several years, one or two of us felt his ego was getting carried away. Outwardly he was very successful and charming, and as a result he received much well-deserved praise, but that encouraged a more self-absorbed attitude. In a roundabout way, Chetan mentioned the situation to the Master. The Master looked unruffled and was completely poised. After a while the Master said, 'Sometimes we have to wait for someone's ego balloon to burst. It is the nature of pride and ego that they ultimately fall in on themselves.' It happens all the time that we can get carried away by the ego – but the universe has a way of providing a check. No one is immune; we all have to learn from this experience.

"As you know from reading the Mahabharata, how many times Sri Krishna used to smash the pride of his dearest disciple Arjuna. Many times, Arjuna thought he was the greatest archer, the greatest seeker, the greatest devotee. But, just as frequently, how often Sri Krishna would smash the pride of his dearest devotee. Alas, we don't always have an Avatar like Lord Krishna to directly smash our pride, so it takes a little longer. But the law of karma is inexorable."

"Thank you, Bahir. I like your philosophy. Only I sometimes wish our Master was still in the physical to smash our pride and ignorance."

"When the Master was in the physical, it is true, outwardly he would often scold us and you felt this really accelerated the progress of both the individual scolded and the whole Ashram. But we have to feel the Master's presence is still there in a very tangible way – not just with the beautiful meditative consciousness in the Ashram, but also the reality that the Master is there in spirit looking over our actions, words and motives. If we try to be receptive, the Master will definitely be there to illumine our pride – we just have to listen a little more carefully. But, at the same time as we learn to listen more carefully for the Master's nudges, hints and scoldings, we will become inwardly stronger and closer to him as a result."

"Well, this is marvellous. I'm now inspired to go and give Henry a long lecture on this philosophy. I'm sure he will appreciate it!" said Daniel.

"Excellent idea. Let me know how it goes!" said Bahir.

GETTING NEW DISCIPLES

"Hi Alex, you look quite serious, what's up?" said Bahir.

"Well, we are giving meditation courses, but we are not getting many people to come," replied Alex.

"Yes," said Bahir, "if there is one thing I remember our Master frequently talking about, it is how he valued us offering people the opportunity to learn about meditation and the spiritual life. He wanted us to offer these lectures in an unconditional spirit – without the expectation of getting new members – but at the same time, he would definitely encourage us to try and grow. The Master always wants us to be of service to more seekers."

Alex replied, "Well, we could definitely benefit from welcoming new seekers. That new energy and aspiration would do wonders for the Ashram."

Bahir paused, and then said, "I think you already have the first requirement, which is just to be open to the idea of welcoming new seekers and new members. Our Master was aware of human nature, which can become easily complacent and static. When we have this willingness to grow, expand and welcome new seekers, it shows our heart is open, and the Master really values this."

Alex replied, "Yes, but I'm not sure everyone else in the Ashram has this same willingness to expand. They do not always feel the inner necessity of growing."

"Yes," said Bahir, "but it will always be like this. We can't expect everyone to be interested in all aspects of our manifestation. People come to the Ashram for different reasons. I remember many years ago at another Ashram, Dilip was asking the Master about a disciple who was very quiet and concentrated on meditation. The Master replied that not everyone makes the same promise to the Supreme. Some souls come for the Master's light; some souls come to manifest that light. We shouldn't judge everyone from our own perspective."

"Perhaps some forget their promise to the Supreme," said Alex.

"Well," said Bahir, "I think we all forget the promises of our soul! I get the feeling that in Heaven it is very easy for the soul to make promises, but on earth – well, it's a very different matter! Our Master would often speak about the divine potential he saw and the lofty promises made by our souls. Also, one thing I remember, the Master once said that all it takes is for one really inspired individual to carry a whole Ashram. Don't wait for others, you can just be that inspired individual. If you feel 100% responsible for the success of the Ashram, then you can really make it happen."

Bahir continued, "Going back to your question, you have the aspiration to grow the Ashram, which is the most important starting point. But I feel you also have a little frustration because it is a challenging task. Try to let go of that frustration and don't expect anything from other people. Instead, try to concentrate on all the good things you are doing to try and offer the Master's light. This aspiration is a rare and valuable offering: it is something the world sorely needs. Don't beat yourself up because it is difficult."

"I know you are right, Bahir," said Alex, "but it would still be nice to get more people coming to our lectures. I even memorise all your best jokes and I feel they deserve a bigger audience."

"Oh well, Alex," said Bahir, "perhaps we have identified where you're going wrong – drop my jokes and you may get a better return!"

Alex smiled and said, "What would the Master say about getting more seekers to meditation classes and lectures?"

Bahir replied, "The Master would value both the inner attitude and the outer hard work. The inner prayer and inner willingness are important. As our Master said, 'Imagination has its own power.' The mind has a power to create. If we always think of problems and how difficult it is, that is what we tend to create in reality. If we imagine outer success – welcoming new seekers, imagining the Ashram doing well – then this imagination power helps in creating the right energy."

"Secondly, there is no substitute for hard work – you can't rely on good wishes and inner prayer alone! Putting up posters, doing the hard leg work – many times in the past, how much I really enjoyed these simple activities. It can be very rewarding. When our Master had big concerts and big lectures, how hard we would work – I can't believe it now, we really threw ourselves into postering for quite a few weeks."

Alex replied, "Alas, those days seem to be no more. It's hard to get anyone to go out into town to poster these days. What do you think to paying companies to do the publicity for you?"

"Well, if you have the money, you could try," said Bahir, "but when we tried, the results were always somewhat disappointing. Perhaps it is the way commercial companies work, but perhaps also a reflection of the inner attitude. We want to use our money power, then take relaxation. When we work hard ourselves, we put more of that inner energy into the project and that adds a lot more."

Bahir continued, "The spirit with which we work is important. I remember on one occasion many disciples were working on a project, but the outer results were disappointing. The Master later commented that many of us had an attitude of seeing it as a holiday – having a bit of fun. There was no intensity or soulfulness behind the efforts. Also, there were other times when a project had a disharmony between those working on the project and, of course, this negatively impacted the outer result."

Alex said, "Yes, I've realised that if someone doesn't really want to be there – if their heart is not in a project – it is best if they concentrate on something else."

Bahir replied, "Yes, when the Master was in the physical, he had the capacity to energise our half-hearted efforts into something very intense and focused. And when you got into that 100% effort, you realised how much satisfaction you could get. You also realised everything was possible."

Bahir continued, "It reminds me of a story. I remember on one occasion, the Master asked my old friend Gopal to arrange for 20 university professors to come and meet him. And we thought, 'O God, this is so difficult!' Academic professors are so proud – why would they want to meet a spiritual Master who didn't even have a high-school exam certificate? Anyway, we send off many letters and try to follow through, but nothing – hardly any response. We tell the Master of our difficulties – perhaps hoping for a little sympathy at the scale of the task. But the Master just says, 'If you don't get 10 professors within 5 days, I will cancel the visit.' We hoped for more time, but the Master gave us less! Anyway, we don't want the Master to cancel his visit, so we ask Abhilash to come over. Now Abhilash has no degree – a high school dropout! The perfect person for speaking with distinguished professors. But Abhilash has boundless confidence and faith in our Master. So he comes and we ask, 'What is your plan? We have no idea.' He says, 'Let's go to the university.'"

"So, we literally go knocking on the doors of university professors. Now I happen to be a graduate, so inwardly I'm thinking, 'You're not really supposed to do this.' But fortunately, I keep my mouth shut. As the Master says, 'Never shut down inspiration.' To my great surprise, plus gratitude, the professors are intrigued and are inspired to meet the Master. They warm to Abhilash's sincerity, enthusiasm and cheerfulness. We exceed our Master's minimum request and the visit is a huge success. I could never have envisaged it, but it happened."

"It's great to hear the background of the story," said Alex.

"Yes, it brings back great memories," said Bahir. "The Master could open up so many doors – doors you would assume would remain always closed."

There was a pause and then Bahir said, "Now, I've forgotten what we were talking about."

Alex smiled and said, "Getting people to come to our meditation lectures."

"Ah, yes!" continued Bahir. "I suppose knocking on people's doors isn't much cop these days."

Alex looked pensive and asked, "Our Master valued traditional methods of contacting people – speaking on the phone, posters, leaflets – but the world has changed so much in the past five decades. It's nearly all digital, less room to put up posters, people are reluctant to speak on the phone – only message. How do we reconcile the Master's wishes with the modern reality?"

"Yes, that's the question," said Bahir with a smile, "I have been thinking about that for the past 40 years. In fact, I have often meditated on this question, hoping to hear an inner answer to this dilemma of how to adapt the spiritual life to changes in society. The problem is that after asking the question and going deep within, I never heard a particularly clear answer. So, this is the proof; I always said I was no good at prayer and meditation! Some people think about it once and get a very clear and definitive answer. I admire their receptivity and certainty. Perhaps I think about things too much. But on the other hand, when I ask other questions, I often do get an inner feeling about which direction to take. Maybe the lack of certainty – the lack of a clear answer – is actually the Master's way of answering."

Bahir continued, "To the end of my days, I will always feel the spiritual value of so-called old-fashioned methods of communication. Whatever modern science achieves in terms of speed and efficiency, electronic communication cannot transfer the consciousness of the heart in the way that the human voice can."

"Yes," said Alex, "it always feels an effort to make phone calls, as people are sometimes reluctant to answer. But when I do speak to seekers, it is always much more inspiring and meaningful than relying on text. The problem is that if we insist on using phone, we don't get as many enquiries. People aren't used to this mode of communication anymore."

"Yes, this is the difficulty," said Bahir. "It is great to use the ways the Master preferred, but if you are getting very few phone enquiries – if you are not getting many people to come – what do you do? It would be interesting to ask the same question in the light of changing society and see how the Master would respond. But we can't, so it's hard to know."

Bahir continued, "I feel there are different ways of answering this question and dilemma. The first way is to say: let us take the route of the divine hero. If the Master says to do it one way, let us make it work. It reminds me of a story – shortly before Sri Ramakrishna's mahasamadhi, he expressed a desire to eat an amalaki fruit. All his disciples said, 'But Master, this fruit is out of season – it is impossible to get at this time of the year.' However, one disciple – Nag Mahashay – said to himself, 'The Master has asked for the fruit, so it must be possible.' Without saying anything, Nag Mahashay slipped away and spent three days looking for the fruit. Finally, he found one and brought it back to his Master. Sri Ramakrishna was so happy and, commented on what a great amalaki fruit it was. In this way the Master illumined his disciples on what real faith can do.

"It is like the university professors – we thought it impossible, but it happened. These days I usually think people won't take leaflets – they don't believe anything unless it comes to their computer. This is the so-called progress! But one experience I remember – my old friend Lochan was handing out leaflets in the street and no one was taking them. He was discouraged and wanted to go come home, but he was inspired to meditate first. In this short meditation, he felt his Master's light very strongly, so he thought he should leaflet for another 10 minutes. And literally everything changed – he couldn't give out leaflets quickly enough. Everyone took. So, if we have faith in the Master's grace, everything is possible. I remember once somebody told the Master, 'It is very difficult to get more seekers to our lectures,' and the Master replied, 'Don't insult your soul.' I can't remember the rest of the answer but that phrase seemed to be enough for me! Our mind sees difficulties; our soul sees divine possibilities."

"That sounds very inspiring," said Alex, "but I'm not sure I have the level of faith and devotion of Nag Mahashay."

Bahir replied, "If you were having this conversation with Hanuman or Nag Mahashay they might say, 'Have more faith, stop making excuses, don't think – just do!' But alas, you are not to speaking to them – only a hopeless disciple like me, and, as it happens, I am often sailing in the same boat as you. So, this is the second way of answering the question.

"I feel the Master wanted us to use traditional methods for the benefit of our aspiration and the aspiration of seekers. If we get many seekers by sending a mass email to everyone in town, we are more likely to become inwardly lazy. We would lose that precious aspiration and willingness to work, which is essential for our spiritual life. If we can speak to seekers on the phone, we touch their heart in a way we can't do with an impersonal email. What do we do if we're trying to use the traditional methods but there's no one to ring, and hardly anyone to come to our classes? I don't think our Master would want to make a religion of rules. We need to have some adaptability to changes. We can't expect new seekers to understand the Master's philosophy before they have even started to meditate. If I was born 60 years later, how would I look for information? Probably the same way everyone else does – using smart-computer and internet. Maybe if it were destiny, I would see the Master's posters and feel something.

But I can imagine not believing in the phone or not understanding the value of speaking in person. Since our Master is not physically here to ask, we have to use an inner judgement based on an understanding of what the Master said and why."

Alex replied, "But, if we start adapting rules, is there not a danger we will start to diverge in many different areas?"

Bahir said, "Yes, that is definitely possible and perhaps already happening. We want to be true to the spirit of the Master's teachings, but not always rigid in the outer forms. We may feel the necessity of adapting to changes in society, but we shouldn't use that as an excuse just to please ourselves and forget the spirit of the Master's teachings. How do we draw the line and decide what is the right way forward? Well, it is inevitable disciples will have slightly different interpretations – we can't expect everyone to see the path in the same way."

Bahir said, "But, one thing I should add before I forget. Look at Itsuki in Tujukistan. In his Ashram, he does everything the Master requested – not just in a selected field that appeals to him, but literally everything. In his case, it is all cheerful obedience. He just makes things work because he is all faith in his Master. It is remarkable what he has achieved and the way he does it. We really have a Hanuman in our midst – who would have thought it possible? And look how they have a thriving Ashram. If we want to grow our Ashram, let's go to this model Ashram in Tujukistan and capture some of that infectious spirit."

Alex said, "I've enjoyed our mammoth talk, but I'm still not sure what the answer is!"

"Me, neither!" said Bahir. But I'm glad there is at least one person in the Ashram who has the patience to listen to me. You might not believe it, but this is the condensed version. I could write a book – but who wants to read? We have to keep things in perspective. The Master did want us to reach out to as many seekers as we could, but the means by which we achieve this is also very important to the Master. For now, we have to follow our heart and do the best we can."

Bahir continued, "But, to go back to your question, never give up! Keep trying with giving meditation classes. Don't worry about the outer results; just feel you are sowing seeds, which may germinate now or in the future. We can have no idea how our lectures and meditation can be offering something inwardly very valuable to people. Just one final thing that comes to me. Once a disciple told the Master that they were making great efforts but getting no outer reward. The Master smiled and said, 'Yes, but your efforts are bearing great fruit in another country!' No inner aspiration or inner effort is wasted; Mother Earth definitely needs our prayers and meditations."

Alex added, "Yes, that is true. It reminds me of the Master's story about the time when he was giving a lecture in his very early years, and no one came. But he still gave the lecture and said the walls were very receptive."

"Yes," said Bahir, "that has happened to a few spiritual Masters. But, at the same time, the Masters need more than receptive walls to grow their mission."

THE MODEL ASHRAM

"Bahir, Could you tell us more about Itsuki's Ashram in Tujukistan?" said Alex.

"Well, I recommend speaking to Itsuki directly – or even better, visiting the Ashram itself. Once I sent a simple message asking about an unimportant subject, but Itsuki took the time to ring back and we got talking about how he was looking after the Ashram. It sounded very good, and before I knew it, he had invited me to spend three months there. It was a great experience."

"So how does it compare to our local Ashram?" asked Alex.

"Well comparison is hard – it is a different culture – but one thing I felt quite strongly was the sense of family. It was more than just community, but a spiritual family – with disciples taking an interest in how others were doing. There was an effort to move forward with harmony and goodwill. Outwardly, they are not doing the most striking things, but you feel everything is built on a solid foundation of goodwill and humility, to try and follow the spirit of the Master's path. It is not a rigid adherence to formula, but a joyful attitude to being able to share the Master's path with the world. A reflection of this ethos was in the many activities the Ashram organised throughout the week. Perhaps it would be music or manifestation activities, and often something new, inventive and spontaneous. Also, it was nice to see different activities were organised by a variety of people – even relatively new disciples had come forward to be involved in a particular aspect of the Ashram."

"That sounds good," said Alex, "I would love more disciples in our Ashram to come forward and take responsibility for various aspects."

"Yes, Itchenko has a knack of giving disciples the sufficient support and encouragement to follow the aspect of the Master's path that appeal to them. With this goodwill, he is able to also gently steer the direction of projects so they keep the spirit of the path."

At this point, a big chap with a large smile on his face entered the café. Eyeing up Bahir and Alex, he confidently strode towards their table. He pulled up a chair, sat down and with a commanding voice said, "We're all doomed, Bahir!"

Bahir smiled, but did not say anything. Undaunted, Donald continued, "The economy is set to crash. It's all a big Ponzi scheme!" Donald looked excited and ordered a coffee from the waiter.

"It's always good to see you, Donald" said Bahir, "though I've no idea what you're talking about!"

"Well, I'll tell you," continued Donald, needing little encouragement. "It's the level of the borrowing in the economy. The government is encouraging us to take on more and more debt. It's all going to crash and the only people who will benefit will be the big banks, like usual! You can't believe anything you hear on ..."

"Oh dear! Well, I say!" said Bahir. "I suppose when you get to my age, you don't have to worry too much about all that."

"It's all a scam," continued Donald with growing intensity. "You want to read what Peter Jones writes in the Observer about the damage to our economy. Do you not agree, Bahir?"

"Well, it's not quite my cup of tea really," said Bahir. "Fortunately or unfortunately, I've never understood economics properly. Actually, we were just talking about Itsenko's Ashram in Tujukistan which seems to be doing very well, despite the economic difficulties of their country."

"We have to get our money into gold, it's the only safety in these times of crisis!" continued Donald.

"Well, this is the advantage of not having any money," chirped in Alex. "You don't have to worry about where to put it!"

"Yes," said Bahir, "I've never really wanted to understand the world of economics and finance."

"Did the Master ever talk of economic systems?" asked Alex.

"Not as far as I know," said Bahir. "The Master seemed to suggest everything sprang from the inner state of humanity. If we have an outer greed, then the outer economic system seems more prone to these bubbles and crashes. But if humanity were to become genuinely spiritual, then whatever economic or political system we have, it will work. Sri Vijamananda once said something interesting: 'Anarchism would work for the beginning and ending of evolution.'"

"How does that work?" asked Donald.

"Well, I'm not entirely sure," said Bahir, "but when humanity is imperfect and selfish, we need rules, regulations and a degree of government intervention, to stop us taking those selfish actions which harm others. However, if we become aware of our real Self, we feel that whatever we do to others, we are actually doing to our larger Self. If we know who we really are, will we pollute the earth to make a short-term profit? To a person of limited awareness: if we cause harm to the environment, it is out of sight, out of mind. But when we live in the enlarged Self, we are conscious of every living thing. When we are realised, we will always consider the well-being of every sentient being. Then we no longer need rules and regulations, because we only want to do God's Will, which is all harmony and selflessness."

"So, you mean that when everyone realises God, we won't need any rules in the Ashram?" asked Alex with a smile.

"Yes, absolutely," said Bahir. "You won't even need an Ashram leader to tell people what to do!"

"Well, I like the sound of that!" said Donald.

"Yes," said Bahir, "you should hurry up and realise God. A man of your capacity and intensity can easily do it in ten years – if you put your mind to it."

"Just think, Donald," said Alex, "when you realise God, you'll have all that occult knowledge to know exactly what is going on in the world!"

Bahir laughed, "Yes. Though if you experience the infinite ecstasy of nirvana, you may lose interest in the perilous state of the world economy."

"What are you saying?" said Donald with a big smile. "That I spend too long talking about economics and politics?"

"You think I'm joking about realising God in 10 years?" said Bahir. "To quite a few disciples, the Master said, 'You can definitely realise God in this incarnation if you channel your intensity into pleasing the Master at every moment.'"

Donald replied, "So how did it work out for you, Bahir? Did you ever get close in your 60 years?"

"Oh no," said Bahir, "I'm just grateful to have been able to stay on the spiritual path for 60 years. The Master never said I should try to realise God in this incarnation. He knew what he was dealing with! But in your case Donald, I can see you have the potential. You have the fiery determination, the will-power and boundless capacities to fly far beyond the snares of the world."

"I always enjoy your flattery very much Bahir," said Donald, "but what do you think it is going to happen to the future of the world? What did the Master say?"

"I don't know," said Bahir. "Second- or third-hand, I heard different things: sometimes predictions that the world would go through difficult times; sometimes I heard the world would ultimately become very spiritual and the Master's light would be widely accepted. You can take your pick, but it is probably a combination of the two.

"But whilst I heard many other predictions third- or fourth-hand, one experience I remember first hand. We were sitting with the Master, and an older disciple was reading the pages of a financial newspaper. When the Master saw this, he was not happy. It inspired the Master to give a short talk where the Master said we should not worry about the future, but have more faith in God; more faith in our Master. He said it is actually an insult to the Master to always be worrying about our future. We have to live in the present moment; the future will come soon enough. If we buy stocks and shares hoping to beat the market, we will be caught by constant uncertainty and concern over money. Better to simply put any savings in a bank."

"Or gold!" said Donald.

"Or spend less time working!" said Alex.

"So, Donald," said Bahir, "we were just recently talking about a model Ashram. What would you consider to be an important part of the model Ashram?"

"Well, bigger and better prasad for a start. I don't believe in these tiny, cardboard biscuits. I would give homemade organic ice cream, kombucha tea and jam donuts for every prasad," said Donald.

"Excellent," said Bahir. "See, you have intuitively understood the Master's philosophy! The Master was always asking for bigger and better prasads. When it came to prasad, the Master wanted to give joy, not austerity. Once someone asked the Master how we can grow the Ashram. The Master replied, 'Give abundant prasad.' Now, the Master maybe said this with a smile, but at the same time, the Master did really value prasad."

"What about prasad in Tujukistan?" asked Alex.

"What impressed me was the care and thought that they put into making the prasad. They would spend time baking cakes, preparing patisseries or handwritten cards of the Master's writings. You felt they really put their heart into it and this made it very special. Also, when they took prasad it was with great devotion. It helped me to bring back memories of taking prasad by hand from the Master. This same devotional attitude we have to feel – the Master is always there. This is what we have to feel…"

"Right, I'm off to buy some ice cream for prasad!" said Donald.

"Excellent. I always said you were the best disciple in the Ashram," said Bahir.

Donald smiled, took his coffee and dashed out of the café. There was a welcome pause while Alex and Bahir caught their breath after the energy of Donald.

"Well, I liked how you managed to steer the conversation away from the economic crisis" said Alex.

"Yes, it's a useful skill to have. Change the conversation without confrontation," said Bahir.

"But is it true you don't know anything about economics?" asked Alex.

"Well, the thing is," Bahir replied, "when disciples bring up economics – or at least political economics – I feel my life-energy draining away, so I temporarily suffer from a mental blank. Sometimes ignorance is bliss!"

"It's better to be peaceful than to win an argument," said Alex.

"Yes," said Bahir, "I lost interest in arguments many years ago. It is always futile and doesn't do anything for my digestion. But although I jest about Donald realising God, sometimes there is truth in humour. He has so much capacity and energy – it's that kind of volcanic energy which can take you very far in the spiritual life."

"Though it needs some steering," said Alex.

"Yes," said Bahir, "and that's why you are in the wonderful position of Ashram leader, to keep our good disciples on track. Donald has a few rough edges and he really should give up lecturing people on economics, but also I see some very strong divine qualities. If he can keep on the right rails, so to speak, he is a real asset to the Ashram."

"Going back to the Ashram in Tujukistan, are there any other aspects worth mentioning?" asked Alex.

"Yes. Well Donald reminds me of another. There are quite a

few characters in the Ashram, and Itsuki has the awareness to allow these differences to flourish – but flourish in a way that is not disharmonious. Itsuki understands the importance of real devotion and how this might be expressed in different ways. It is an Ashram where you can feel yourself, but also be inspired to put more energy into the spiritual life.

CHAT GROUPS

"Why do you not participate in our message groups?" asked Alex.

"It's not entirely the case," replied Bahir. "There was a time when I found myself added and so I stayed in the background for a while – there is an anxiety of missing out on something important. The problem is that seeing these message groups created an uneasy feeling – something I couldn't quite put my finger on. It was a visceral reaction more than anything."

"What do you mean by 'visceral'?" asked Alex.

"Visceral means a deep-seated, instinctive reaction. It's not a logical thought-out process, but something that comes from within." replied Bahir.

"You mean it is like when Bahir gets up to give a lecture, some disciples feel a visceral desire to get up and quietly slip away?" said Alex.

"Yes! Something like that!" said Bahir.

"But why this reaction? It seems people are only trying to stay in contact." asked Alex.

"Firstly, the Master did not value the impersonal electronic communication. The Master valued meeting in person and the communication which uses the human voice, because then you can express a range of emotions and touch the heart of the other person."

"It is good to remember the Master's philosophy of the heart and his views on technology, but people say the world has changed so much," said Alex.

"It is true the world has changed, but I'm not sure that emulating the world is something we should be striving for. The material world is changing beyond recognition, but the world is also struggling. Even many in the secular world feel our ever-increasing reliance on electronic devices has an adverse impact on issues like concentration, personal self-esteem and happiness."

"Some might say this particular technology was not around when the Master was in the body, so how do we actually know?" said Alex.

"It is true to some extent, but the spirit of the Master's teachings are more important than very specific examples. Different types of electronic communication over the internet have tended to merge into one. To understand the Master's philosophy, just observe the difference between speaking in person and sending messages. Also, there is a very different dynamic between sending a message to an individual and sending to a whole group at once. It becomes like a more powerful version of e-mail.

"Like anything, it depends how it is used, but sometimes I feel the sacred is merging into the superficial," said Bahir. "The medium is OK for sharing factual information – times of concert etc. – but when you share the Master's most lofty experiences and people reply with comments, to me it carries nothing of the sacred reality and is quite jarring.

"The Master said the more you use technology, the more other capacities will diminish. When a dear disciple passes or there is some other very significant news, it sometimes gets put on a message group. This kind of thing should be shared in person or on the phone, but when we are accustomed to posting to message groups, we don't use the so-called old-fashioned methods of communication, and we lose out on the valuable human interaction. We can gain an unending stream of messages and hundreds of online friends, but inwardly we can still feel isolated, because the heart – the psychic being – is not being fed. The Master once gave a talk where he said the spiritual life is all about the heart – we need to feed and strengthen the heart, our intuition, the psychic part of us. But when we use machines we are actually moving away from this reality."

"But isn't it OK if we just limit to basic information or a very limited purpose?" asked Alex.

"Yes, maybe," said Bahir. "There are some groups that are used only to share the times of rehearsals or something like that. Also, if people just send a daily aphorism, perhaps that is OK too. I much prefer to read the Master's writings on paper, but some like to receive something on their phone. However, if you have a group 'general inspiration', the nature of the technology means it is easy for the purpose to evolve and grow. Every year Thomas says we need to be stricter in keeping the Ashram group to a limited purpose. But this intention lasts just a few weeks until – as if pulled by an invisible force – the group expands to more and more messages, and these messages come unmoderated. When it's so easy to post, it's also easy to post something that is maybe a little inappropriate."

"But," said Alex, "some people say they just use message groups for sharing inspiring news, and that this is a useful service, especially for those who live in isolated communities."

"There are different ways message groups can be used. And if people feel it is a really positive influence in their lives, then they will continue to use. Some people do seem to really like them. They don't have to listen to an old man like me! The only thing I would add is that good news can be even more valuable if it is shared in person or on the phone. A disciple once said that hearing about our spiritual retreat through speaking on the phone, they could feel a little bit of the Master's light from the disciple who had just returned and was sharing the news. This light doesn't come through electronic text. I like to see good news too, but it is a shame if we rely only on the electronic means and do not speak to people as much as we used to.

"It reminds me: a few years ago, I was reading some notes of a disciple who lived in the very early years of the Master. If the Master achieved anything significant, there would be a chain of telephone calls, so everyone would be kept in the loop. The comment in the diary was something like, 'The phones were dancing through the night. It felt like a spiritual party.' The excitement of receiving phone updates and sharing in the achievements of the Master can never be adequately understood by those who did not experience it. Those golden days are now buried in oblivion. It is almost impossible to revive that tradition of chain phone-calls. It is from another age. But the Master knew how much joy and inspiration it gave, and that is why he tried in vain to encourage its use."

"With message groups, isn't it useful for irregular visitors to the Ashram to keep informed and feel that they are in the loop?" said Alex.

Bahir replied, "Once Virat was travelling in Myanmar and there was a beautiful Buddhist temple where locals would come when they felt like it, to meditate with the monks. Back home, Virat asked the Master if we could do something similar for seekers who didn't want to join but who wanted to have an occasional meditation. The Master said, 'No.' If you offer an easier version of the path – with little commitment – many will choose the easier drop-in version. That is human nature, but the soul wants something higher. The point is that if people don't come regularly, I don't feel we are particularly helping them by giving a bit of electronic chat and a few photos to see. I feel it works the other way. If people have this easy option of reading and posting to chat groups, over time they may feel less necessity in the actual, real spiritual practice of attending meditation and speaking to disciples. If someone is ill, definitely you should make an effort to keep in touch. You can speak on the phone or even send messages if you prefer, but I don't see the necessity of making it a group experience. People will value it much more if it is personalised rather than just an impersonal post to everyone.

"Last week, I was participating in the sacred walk past the Master's statue. The person in front of me was filming this sacred moment with their phone. It disturbed my attempts to be soulful. I guess he wanted to record and post for the benefit of his fellow monks who couldn't come to the main Ashram. You could say it comes from a motivation to think of others. But no matter how beautiful the video, it doesn't capture the inner stillness – the inner consciousness – of the Master. A friend once said something funny and profound, 'The best thing in the world is coming to our spiritual retreat. The worst thing in the world is watching the spiritual retreat on extended highlights!'

"It's hard to explain, but the outer form is only 1% of the experience. I remember when the Master was in the physical, he would encourage some singing groups that were really of a poor standard from a musical perspective. But so many experiences we can have when we feel and hear beyond the outer form.

"One other thing that comes to mind: when the Master was in the physical, the Master had disciples who – for various reasons – would never be able to visit our main Ashram to gain darshan of the Master. Disciples researched many ways of setting up a live video link so at least they would be able to see the Master on video. But in response to a live video link, the Master said, 'No, it will ruin their aspiration.' The Master would often set up phone calls for outlying centres, and we would eagerly go to hear the Master speak on speaker phone, but there was never any use of video link-up, even though the technology would have been possible. At the same time, one of the most precious things we have is recorded videos of the Master – especially when he was in those deep meditations. But if we have a live link or a comprehensive set of recordings, people will have less motivation to travel, because they can feel they will get extended highlights at home. The real essence of the spiritual retreat is to be there in person and become absorbed in the indefinable consciousness of the Master.

"But," asked Alex, "in this generation, new seekers are so used to message groups. It comes as second nature. By offering new seekers the opportunity to join a group, we can help them make the transition to Ashram life," said Alex.

"Bringing new seekers into the Ashram and making them feel welcome is a most important and sacred responsibility. I don't want to say how it should be done. Every disciple has to be guided by their inner feeling and meditation. We have to take the opportunity as one of our greatest responsibilities. We have to ask: how can we help them to feel they are part of the Master's family? Having said that, my heart inwardly sinks when one of the first steps of entering the Ashram is to be inducted into a chat group. The question is: do people really get the Master's vibration from being part of these message groups? Does it touch their heart and soul in these precious days of receptivity and willingness to take on new ideas? Furthermore, in my case, it took several years to really understand all the nuances of the Master's path – for example, how to express yourself in a group situation, and communication between male and female disciples. In message groups, there is a subtle pressure in knowing when, how, and what to post and reply.

"One other thing: our path is the path of the heart. By bringing the heart to the fore, we hope to reduce the ego, and diminish our qualities of pride, ego, jealousy and all that. But does this kind of social media really help to bring the heart to the fore? Some use groups to request people to pray for various things, and people respond, 'Yes I will meditate.' But if you make a sacred inner commitment to pray and meditate, do you need to broadcast this to a chat group? When you're with friends you can chat about cabbages and kings into the early hours of the morning – you can say just about anything, and the joy and light in your eyes will convey infinitely more. But in a message group the mind is quietly judging everything: 'Why did she like his photo but not mine? If everyone else is making a commitment to meditate, what am I supposed to do?' If our photos are getting feedback, perhaps we get drawn into seeking that dopamine hit from people viewing our posts. After functions – even during prasad – sometimes we instinctively check our phones to see whether people have viewed our messages, or we post updates from the function. This is not how to assimilate a good meditation. Social media can take us out of the present moment and we lose that 100% absorption in what the Master is trying to give us.

"The Master once said something quite profound. He was asked whether it was easier to aspire in the modern age. He said: no – in the modern age, it was much harder, for two reasons. Firstly, we are bombarded with information. Even when the mind is full, we still want to feed the mind more and more. How often throughout the day do we hear the beep of phones announcing new messages? It can weaken the subtle nerves and subconsciously we feel tied to the machines. We have to drop everything to see what it is. At the very least, we can turn off instant notifications and check only once or twice a day. Sometimes we are chatting with people, and at the same time they are distracted by a notification – even reading the message at the same time as conversing.

"The second difficulty the Master mentioned is that when we do anything, we are always looking around to see if other people are noticing what we are doing. These two difficulties that the Master mentioned many years ago are the essence of social media and chat groups. And yet they are very addictive to human nature, so they hold a pull over us. If spiritual seekers cannot be free of this constant electronic communication, what hope for the rest of the world?"

"Don't you think you might be overthinking it all?" asked Alex.

"Yes, absolutely!" said Bahir. "Many hours I have tortured myself over this question. It is perhaps a shame I didn't use that time for something more constructive! It is a powerful tool when you can share with 100 people all at once. With this kind of forum, it is easy to push well-meaning ideas. But in the haste and convenience of sending so many messages to so many people, these ideas may not have quite the desired impact, and may cause new problems.

"When starting new projects," continued Bahir, "it is important to start from the proper basis. This means talking in person and gaining an understanding of what people are happy with. Even good projects can go wrong if they start on message groups and we don't get the right kind of collective energy. The curse of electronic communication is that it is so easy to have misunderstandings. Once Pankuja spoke to the Master about internet forums. The thing he remembered was the dreadful look of suffering and pain on the Master's face as the Master's inner vision saw all the hostile forces that lurk around internet forums. True, our forums exclude outside people and mostly focus on good news, but used like a chat group, they can still trigger certain emotions. It is easy to have misunderstandings – and even arguments – when all we do is type.

"Also, there is an issue of effectiveness. Sometimes you give 'inspiring messages' on our Ashram forums. The intention is good, but you lose nearly everything by posting on this medium. It is just another notification out of hundreds. It's so easy to ignore. In spirituality, it is not the words we say but the inner force behind them that matters. If you speak in person, people will pick up on your cheerfulness and the joy in your face. If you carry the Master's consciousness, people will follow you – even if your words are limited and the project is not the greatest. But on a message group, none of this comes across. It is barren: no heart; only words on a screen.

"Usually it is a great joy to talk with you Bahir," said Alex, "but today it is all seriousness and gloom. Haven't you told us not to look at what others do and let them make their own choices?" asked Alex.

"How I wish I could follow my own advice!" said Bahir. "But the nature of these groups means it does affect everyone – even those who are left out. And there are other disciples who feel the same misgivings."

Bahir paused as if becoming more reflective.

"One thing I could add: I once went to a foreign Ashram where they use message boards with a certain moderation. It only felt like a minor aspect of their Ashram – they do so many inspiring things together and there is great oneness amongst the disciples, so this gave me an important perspective. Before I went, I thought I might mention it, but when I was there having a good time, I thought, 'Why bother?' Everybody needs to choose their path across the river. We are all just travelling in slightly different boats – trying to be happy in our own way.

"When you have got very used to something, it's very hard to jump into another boat. That is why I don't think it is worth trying to change anyone's mind on this subject. When I joined the spiritual path, many years ago, it was a much simpler, pre-internet age. I look back on those days with tremendous fondness; the Master was in the physical, and we waited on his every talk and message with bated breath. But it is difficult to retain that intensity. Things change.

"I would prefer if functions and meditations were free of phones, but even despite the distractions I sometimes meditate better in a group than in perfect silence on my own. It makes no sense, but that is fine with me!"

"Well, all this certainly gives me plenty of material for our next webchat," said Alex with a smile.

"Yes, that would be a very effective way to let everyone know!" said Bahir. "Whether there is any truth in all this, I don't know. Everyone is trying to do the right thing. But if you get in a sticky situation, don't rely on electronic communication. Try speaking. The Master didn't just say all that for the benefit of philosophy. It does make a difference."

FAVOURITE ASPECT OF THE MASTER

"Hi Reynash, what is your favourite aspect of the Master's Path?" asked Bahir.

"I'm not sure," replied Reynash, "but I suppose the one thing that really matters is the Master's love for his disciples. Everything else is a manifestation of this reality. And because of this love, he is willing to do anything for us."

"What do you mean by that?" Asked Bahir.

Reynash replied, "Well, it means the Master is always willing to protect and encourage our spiritual progress. Often, we want the Master to fulfil our desires – but what can he do? We are praying for the Master to fulfil our outer desires, but the Master has made a promise to the Supreme to lead us towards our liberation. When I say the Master would do anything for his disciples, it means he is willing to try and illumine our ego.

"Let me tell you a story, which is illumining, though not always easy to tell. When I had been a disciple several years, I was quite happy in the spiritual life. I felt my life had been transformed and it was a lot of fun spending time with my brother disciples. I didn't always take the Master's words to heart, but I felt I was doing enough. Any spiritual life seemed much better than my former life, which was all confusion. The Master gave so much; we took what we wanted and also pleased ourselves to a considerable extent. Anyway, there was an occasion when the Master invited spiritual questions, so I asked the Master, 'What can we do to help your mission the most?' The Master replied, 'To help my mission the most, you can leave the Ashram.'

"Well, I was stunned. Not in a million years did I expect this. So many thoughts raced around my mind: 'Did my Master mean it literally? What is the meaning behind this answer?' The Master left the meeting and I retreated in embarrassment to my room, trying to work out what was going on. Now, a little later my old friend Gopal comes and asks how I am doing and will I be joining the later meditation? So, I tell Gopal I don't feel like doing anything at the moment, and what am I supposed to make of the Master's answer? Gopal smiles compassionately and says, 'Oh don't worry, Reynash, the Master often says things like that. It is the Master's shock-blessing – trying to shake us out of a complacent attitude to the spiritual life. You may not believe it now, but in the future you may look back and understand the benefit of getting this answer, at this particular time in your life.'

"At the time, I appreciated Gopal's concern, but I was struggling to see it from that perspective. Gopal could see I was quite depressed so he continued talking: 'Reynash, you might find it hard to believe, but it is a really good sign that the Master is willingly to give you that public scolding. How many times the Master has scolded me, but at the same time, how much love the Master has shown. If the Master is willing to scold you, it shows that he feels you have the capacity to take it in a meaningful way and make a change to your spiritual life – a transformation that otherwise might not occur for a very long time. The Master's only real punishment is his indifference.'

"'Reynash, let me tell you a juicy story. Once we were with the Master – just myself and two others. We were speaking to the Master in an informal way and the Master felt free to talk about many juicy topics. Then he became serious and said, 'I have quite a few very good disciples and some third-class disciples who are at least trying to become better. But also I have some unfortunate disciples who are constantly disobeying me, while at the same time they cannot imagine they are doing anything wrong. It has become a hopeless case. These disciples may or may not be outwardly close, but inwardly I have withdrawn. With my universal heart, I love them unconditionally, but I can no longer take immediate responsibility for their spiritual life – it is all disobedience and self-justification. The outer and inner closeness are often two entirely different things. They are sailing in their own boat.'

"Gopal continued, 'This was quite a revelation, so I asked the Master, 'You often scold me for doing wrong things – is this is a sign that I am not a hopeless case?' The Master smiled broadly and said, 'Yes, Gopal. It is true you are not a completely hopeless case! It is true, I often scold you, but I know that you can make unimaginable progress when you take these scoldings in the right spirit. Sometimes you sulk and feel sorry for yourself, and then you do not make any progress, but when you do take my scoldings in the spirit of transformation, how much progress you make.'

"'The Master continued, 'Sometimes disciples ask questions, but already in the back of their minds they have decided what they are going to do anyway. In this case, it would be better not to ask the Master. If you go on your own path, that is one thing. But if you ask the Master and the Master tells you what to do, it is a serious mistake in the spiritual life to then disregard the advice of your spiritual Master and go in the opposite direction.'

"'The Master continued, 'When I was following the spiritual life in India, my own Guru was very strict. He was compassion and justice in equal measure, and we loved the Guru for correcting our spiritual life. But when I made plans to travel to the West, my Guru smiled and said, 'In America, my path of justice-light you will rarely be able to use. In America, you will have to use your compassion-power infinitely more than the justice-aspect.' How prophetic have my Guru's words been! At the same time, I sometimes see that compassion has completely failed and justice-light is the only tool left. When you have a patient, you can try to cure the patient by making them feel comfortable and offer them reassurance, but this can do only so much to make them healthy. Sometimes, for really stubborn diseases, you need to give the patient an injection. The injection is painful for a short while, but it can cure the disease in a way that outer compassion cannot. If you are suffering from a fatal disease, would you prefer the doctor doesn't give you an injection because the needle hurts for a short while?'"

Reynash continued, "I have to say: this was very helpful. I'm very grateful Gopal was there to share this insight into the Master. I even tried to cultivate a little divine pride that I had been scolded by the Master – though this didn't really work. I still felt adrift and I asked myself soul-searching questions. Where was I going in the spiritual life? Was my attitude all wrong? What should I do? A whole range of emotions and thoughts went through my mind. After a few days of rumination and introspection, I was still in something of a rut. But Gopal comes with a message from the Master: 'Where is Reynash? I haven't seen him for a few days. He should go and help Balin with building the wall.'

"So, with a little inner reluctance – almost defiance – I go and help Balin with building the wall. This was a tough job, but it was a good experience, as it helped me get out of the mental doldrums. Balin was a great person to be around. He wasn't into talking philosophy or wasting time in gossip – he was just a dedicated worker. He had boundless energy and willingness to get on with the job, without making a fuss or drama. We worked in near silence, and the work became meditative and fulfilling. Balin was always working for the Master with a good attitude and this significantly helped me to be in a good consciousness.

"So, over the next few weeks, I spent a lot of time with Balin. But also, it felt different. I lost my former complacent feeling – a feeling I didn't even realise that I had. When the Master spoke, I felt inwardly on my toes – trying to take things more seriously and soulfully. I still had many different thoughts going through my mind, but slowly I was rebuilding my spiritual life. At the same time, there was a real newness in it. Every now and then the Master would come to inspect our work. The Master would only speak to Balin, but the Master would offer a blessingful smile to his other workers; in that moment, you remembered the Master's love and inner concern. It is hard to explain the power of the Master's smile; it went straight into your heart and fed your soul and heart like nothing else could. It could stay with you for a considerable time. Even now, I can bring back those precious memories. So slowly, the shock to the system faded, and I realised I was following the spiritual life with new purpose and greater humility. A few months later, out of the blue, the Master offered me a blessing on my birthday, and said a few words that seemed to have tremendous power and blessings. When the Master scolded it was with tremendous sincerity, but when he offered his blessings, they also meant more than ever. I felt it was two sides of the coin – the Master scolded my ego, but as my ego came crashing to the floor, there was this inner wave of love and compassion to bring my devotional heart and soul to the fore.

"There is an old Zen saying that to fill a cup with nectar, it is first necessary to remove the muddy water. The Master wanted to give the nectar so much, he was willing to knock out the dirty water in my mind first. I also realised that working with Balin on these projects for the Master was a real blessing. I realised how much in the past I had been living in the gossip world – criticising other people, but not actually doing very much positive myself. But with Balin there was no time, it was like my half-hearted attitude to the spiritual life had been replaced by a genuinely devoted attitude. So, in many ways, Gopal was right. I can look back and see that outwardly painful experience as a real turning point."

"It is hard to imagine you as a half-hearted disciple, Reynash. You are a real pillar of the Ashram," Said Bahir.

"This is the proof the Master's scolding worked. If the Master had indulged my mind's demands and expectations, where would I be in the spiritual life? But I still feel that the Master is right – his compassion-light he uses ten times more than his justice-light. Outwardly you might just hear the Master's scoldings, but inwardly I felt his love which transformed my life. He uses this infinitely more than his scoldings."

THE AURA OF THE MASTER

"Reynash, you spent a lot of time close to the Master, how was the experience?" asked Bahir.

"Whatever the Master was doing, he had a very special aura. It was like putting half a foot in another world – a world where spirituality was perfectly natural and normal; where every sense and thought was heightened. You could feel tremendously uplifted, while also many things that were lurking in your nature could be brought to the surface for their transformation. I just told you a scolding story, and these tend to make quite good stories! But this is only one particular aspect of the Master. It is harder to recount stories of the innumerable occasions when the Master would be 'dealing with business,' meditating, talking – either seriously or in a light-hearted fashion.

"When the Master was in a soulful mood, it brought your own soulfulness to the fore; when the Master was enjoying humour, it made everything more humorous. It could feel like you were just surfing on the wave of the Master's inner and outer presence. I remember one time when a few of his disciples put on a humorous play about one of the Master's short stories. The Master was enjoying the performance like anything; to see his very serious disciple Arun dressed up like a donkey brought him so much joy. But I remember watching this same play on a recorded video a few months later, and it felt like the magic had gone. Watching in person, with the Master a few metres away, brought you into the Master's consciousness, but watching on tape wasn't the same. I couldn't watch it all because it was such a different experience."

Alex said, "I know what you mean. Some things don't translate so well. Two people can tell the same joke, but with one person it is much funnier," said Bahir.

Bahir continued, "Would you get the chance to ask the Master questions about your own spiritual life?"

"Not very often," said Reynash, "I didn't want to bother the Master with personal questions and my own problems. I always felt the Master had enough problems in the Ashram to be dealing with. But I sometimes asked questions on behalf of friends who lived further away and didn't have easy access to the Master."

"What did you learn from the way the Master answered questions?" asked Bahir.

Reynash replied, "Well you could never predict how the Master would answer, or which questions he would feel were important. Also, sometimes the Master would not give any particular outer answer. Perhaps a friend would mention a particular issue in their life or in the Ashram. The Master would read the written question and then go silent. In that brief moment of meditation, you could feel the Master was inwardly working on the inner reality of the issue."

"Why do you think the Master would remain silent on questions?" asked Bahir.

"Another spiritual Master once said it is not possible to write the biography of a spiritual Master because their real life is on the inner plane – dealing with the soul's world and all the inner forces that shape our outer lives. But once someone asked the Master a similar question to this. From what I remember, the Master said, 'Sometimes, if I offer outer concern and speak to the individual it doesn't help solve that particular problem.'"

Reynash continued, "My understanding is that sometimes, it is not the outer advice we need, but the change in the inner attitude. To resolve problems, we look for outer solutions, but if we can look at the issue with a different perspective, we can definitely solve it. This is what the Master tries to do – offering an inner force, to give disciples the inner capacity to deal with their problems."

Reynash continued, "The Master had an unfailing insight into the lives of his disciples and families. The Master would often speak briefly, but in each word there could be tremendous meaning and value. When you were with the Master, you felt he could see everything that was going on in your spiritual life. If you were sincere, you felt you could not hide anything from the Master – but it was never with a sense of exposure. It felt more like he had a very compassionate and forgiving understanding of human nature. Of course, sometimes you tried to hide things from the Master, but the Master never appreciated this attitude. It is only when we are willing to give up these wrong movements that the Master could work on them."

Reynash continued, "Once, I was worried about my father's health, but as usual I didn't want to bother the Master. However, out of the blue, as if picking up on my inner thoughts the Master asked me, 'How are your parents?' He asked with such affection and concern that I felt silly for not mentioning it. So, I was able to tell the Master my concerns about my father's health. He took it very seriously and wanted to know the time when my father would go for an operation. For the next few days, the Master frequently asked about my father with genuine concern. At the time of my father's operation, the Master said he would offer a very powerful force and concentrate on my father. A few weeks later, my father let slip that during his operation he had seen a very powerful and beautiful light. He didn't really understand, but he felt intuitively it must be due to my 'Guru'. My father rarely talks about spirituality. I don't know what he believes, so to talk about this was quite significant. I was quite moved at the care and attention the Master offered to my father. I felt it was all due to the Master's love for his disciples. If the Master had this kind of care and love for our family members, it illustrates the love that he has for us."

Bahir added, "I have heard from many disciples how the Master would inwardly care for their close family members – especially in that moment of their departure from the earth."

Reynash replied, "Yes, that is true. So many moving stories I heard. To the medical science, these stories would be considered miracles or impossible, but they did happen, and with the Master you started to take for granted that this 'miraculous possibility' was actually the way the world was supposed to be. One funny story that the Master told – and I should add when the Master told these kinds of stories, he would always preface, 'This comes from my imagination – so you can believe or disbelieve.' But anyway, the Master said he was concentrating on the father of a disciple who had passed away. A few days after his death, he was still caught in the lower vital worlds, so the Master occultly travelled to this lower realm and offered to take this disciple's parent to an infinitely higher Heavenly realm. But the father said, 'No thanks. I don't want to leave the vital world – I like it here!' The Master was amazed a soul had wanted to stay in the lower worlds – it had never happened before! It just shows that after death – for most people – we usually end up in a place that is a reflection of our vibration on earth. For people who enjoy constant excitement and the vital life, Heaven can become boring – which is why after a few years, souls reincarnate to try and make more spiritual progress on earth."

"I love these stories," said Bahir.

"Yes. I wish I could remember more," said Reynash. "One interesting anecdote comes to mind. It's not really related to escaping the vital worlds, but never mind!

"I once asked the Master a question: 'How successful have we been in sharing your light to the world?' The Master looked serious and after a brief pause answered, 'In all honesty, only very little of my light has been shared. I feel that my disciples could easily offer much more. At the Ashram restaurant we work hard to share food, but disciples could offer so much more – if they spent a little time talking to our customers, asking how they are, expressing some concern for their lives. The problem is that we think manifestation is some big project, but every moment is an opportunity to touch someone's heart and bring forward their latent spirituality. Even just smiling at people we meet in daily life can have a very positive impact.'

"Perhaps the reason I mention this is that it ties up with the experience of being in the Master's presence. Whatever the Master was doing – be it playing sport, meditation, talking – it was drawing you into his world, it was feeding you inwardly and bringing his spirituality to the fore.

"The only difficulty with spending so much time with the Master was that you could became complacent about the spiritual opportunities you were used to getting every day. Those who lived far afield and travelled a few times a year really treasured the smallest outer connection – and this helped them to be more devotional in the Master's presence."

Bahir replied, "Yes, when I was a new disciple, I used to regret that I wasn't born 20 years early and closer to where the Master's main Ashram was. But, over time, I realise that it was unnecessary. Being born at the particular time and place of my birth was the right thing for me."

"Yes," said Reynash, "and I see that in some of the disciples who have come after the Master's physical passing. It is moving to see their gratitude and devotional feeling of being able to follow in the Master's footsteps – to see the places he visited in person so many years ago. With the right spirit, we can feel the inner presence of the Master in these places. In some cases, they have cultivated more devotion than some of us who were in the Master's physical presence. But at the same time, when I think back to those days of spending time with the Master, I feel all gratitude for the many blessings and opportunities. True, I could have made much more of this opportunity, but it doesn't help to think like this. I believe it was the Master's mission to accept so many of us who were spiritual beginners – perhaps it was to show that the Master's path was accessible to the whole of humanity, and not just very advanced seekers."

"Yes," said Bahir, "when I read about the disciples of Sri Namayananda, it seems they were all the time slipping into samadhi. When I look around our Ashram it is more likely to see disciples slipping off to sleep!" said Bahir.

Reynash smiled, "Yes, there is something in that. Though many years after the event, it is only natural biographers concentrate on the good qualities of disciples. After a thousand years, perhaps future Ashram historians will turn us all into saints too. That would be funny! And I'm sure the Master would laugh the hardest at the idea he was surrounded by saints. But as the Master once said, 'A saint is a sinner who never gave up.'"

"Well Saint Reynash doesn't sound right, does it?" said Bahir. "And as for a halo, the only thing I see around your head is a day's worth of stubble."

"Yes. That is a bit embarrassing. I shall go and get a shave straight away. You caught me unawares. But thanks for listening to my stories this morning." said Reynash.

ACCEPTING DISCIPLE IN THEIR OWN WAY

Kalo was a relative newcomer to his Master's path, and since joining he had been most inspired by those disciples who had been with the Master as far back as the early days of his mission. He felt these disciples had really imbibed part of his Master's light.

There was also a part of him that wished he had been born just a few years earlier, as his Master had a much closer outer relationship with these disciples. Although these thoughts came into his mind, he also just felt grateful to be on the path, and felt his Master really valued the inner connection much more.

In many aspects of the spiritual life, his Guru could be very strict. He set very high standards and gave specific instructions on many things, which were not necessarily printed in his books. Sometimes it was a challenge to live up to these standards. His Master had a remarkable knack for discouraging those options which were easy and convenient for the human mind! But, at the same time, Kalo saw in his Master's teaching the concern and compassion of his Master, who knew all the subtle influences affecting a disciple's consciousness.

One thing Kalo observed was how his Master could treat different disciples in very different ways. To some, the Master would scold for seemingly little rhyme or reason, whilst others would receive the kindest encouragement and highest praise. He felt this was a fascinating aspect of his divine Master – treating each soul according to its needs and capacity, and the Will of the Supreme.

However, sometimes Kalo felt confused when he saw some disciples ignoring the Master's specific wishes. He even started to question whether or not he had understood his Master philosophy properly.

Even more confusingly, on occasion the Master not only seemed to tolerate their behaviour, but also would find ways to encourage and praise these disciples.

After ruminating on this confusion for a few weeks, a chance arose for Kalo to ask his Master. He felt a little nervous, but in a diplomatic manner he asked why the Master tolerated disciples behaving in a way that was contrary to the Master's previous talks.

His Master most compassionately gave a faint smile – a smile that conveyed great pathos and concern. He replied, "What can I do? I have to start by accepting my disciples in their own way – until they are ready to accept me in my own way.

"I encourage them – in the hope they will one day feel the inner necessity of following my path in my own way."

The Master grew more serious. With a penetrating glare, the Master looked into Kalo's eyes and continued, "But from some disciples, I expect no compromise."

It felt like his Master had penetrated into the core of his being. He felt his Master was blessingfully speaking directly to his soul.

The Master's stern face slightly relaxed and he finished, "Of course, each disciple has to decide for themselves what they want. Do they want to please themselves or do they want to please me in my own way?"

Kalo inwardly marvelled at the spiritual depth, compassion and wisdom of his Master. He was literally bursting with joy at the divine opportunities that came from following his Master's path.

STORIES FROM THE SPIRITUAL LIFE, PART 2

THE SMOKING DISCIPLE

Many thousands of years ago, there was a spiritual Master who used to invite all his disciples to an annual spiritual festival for the New Year.

With so many visitors, accommodation and food were basic, but the visiting disciples didn't mind the material – simply because they got so much inspiration from being with their Master and their spiritual brothers and sisters.

Arjun was a relatively new disciple. He was most excited at the opportunity to meditate with his Master and join the Ashram activities. However, one day the Heavens opened and suddenly queuing outside in the rain for lunch wasn't quite so appealing.

As the cold rain started to penetrate his clothes, an old disciple called Tushar took pity on Arjun and said, "You look a bit cold there my friend, how would you fancy a nice bit of warm soup? I have a little place around the corner."

Arjun readily accepted, and he followed Tushar to his room, which was a treasure trove of artefacts and pictures of his Master. It was a little chaotic and messy, but the room had a real feeling of living devotion to the Master. Arjun eyed a framed picture where his Master looked very young, with Tushar by his side. Arjun asked about the picture.

"Yes, that was when the Master first came to Puri, and I worked as the Master's assistant building the first walls of the Ashram."

Tushar proceeded to tell some cute and inspiring stories about his early years – which had illumining insights and Tushar's own unique sense of humour. He would sometimes veer off into complaints about the locals or other disciples, so Arjun worked hard to steer the conversation on to any reminiscence of his Master.

Tushar was happy to have such a good listener in Arjun. In full flow he said, "You know sometimes, Arjun, you can't believe anything disciples tell you. Unless I hear from the lips of the Master, I don't trust! Let me tell you a funny story. There was a time when the Master was asked about his recommendations for food, and the Master replied, 'Well, I really like eggplant and cucumber.'

"And can you imagine what happened? Yes, we had eggplant and cucumber for breakfast, lunch and dinner! Everyone stopped coming to the Ashram food hall, as they couldn't face any more cucumber sandwiches. When the Master found out what was happening, he scolded the cooks like anything. 'Just because I said I liked eggplants and cucumbers, it doesn't mean I expect you to give it at every meal!' You see, Arjun, sometimes disciples hear something from the Master and they interpret it in their own way."

Arjun smiled.

Tushar lent back and casually asked Arjun, "Do you mind if I have a little smoke?"

Arjun nearly jumped out of his chair. He was flabbergasted to see Tushar taking out some tobacco and lighting his pipe. When Arjun joined the Ashram, he was told one of the rules of the Ashram was: no smoking. He was glad of the rule, as he never liked the habit anyway. Now, he was too shocked to say anything.

Tushar opened the window a little and gave a little laugh. He said, "Yes, I know; the Master doesn't really like smoking, but in my case, he gave an exception. I'd like to give it up. I just can't.

"Actually, now I remember – the Master said I can smoke as long as nobody sees me doing it. So, Arjun, good chap, it's probably best not to tell any other disciples. You know what they are like with a bit of gossip!"

Arjun smiled politely, but he kind of felt it was perhaps time to move on. He didn't particularly want his clothes to smell of tobacco.

Arjun finished his soup and made his excuses to leave.

***

Later in the week, he was still thinking about his interesting experiences with Tushar when he met another old disciple called Gopal.

Arjun really appreciated the opportunity to speak with Gopal. He was one of the busiest disciples in the Ashram, but he always made time to talk to anyone, and offer a bit of friendly chat and encouragement.

As Gopal asked Arjun about his stay, Arjun couldn't resist telling him about his meeting with Tushar. "The thing, is Gopal; I didn't know some disciples were allowed to smoke."

Gopal raised his eyebrows, as if momentarily perturbed – a rare divergence from his usual poise. Then he burst out laughing. "Yes, Tushar's a bit of a rogue, but a loveable rogue, I suppose. The Master has his rules, but for his own unfathomable reasons, can choose to break them if necessity demands. He once said: 'Every rule has its exceptions – and even that has its exceptions.'"

Gopal continued, "In Tushar's case, he was incredibly loyal in the early years of the Master's mission, when locals were trying to block the building of the new Ashram. The Master never forgets this kind of devotion and loyalty. So, Tushar's case is special, and the Master does allow him a greater flexibility than he would give to other disciples. However, I have to say, an exception for smoking may only apply in Tushar's case."

With a laugh, Gopal enquired, "I hope you're not thinking of starting to smoke Arjun."

Arjun smiled and mentioned the 'cucumbers for breakfast' story. Gopal laughed again. "Yes, there is truth in that story, though Tushar may have embellished in his own way. But I did wonder why one year we were getting a lot of cucumbers for breakfast!"

Gopal continued, "It is true; disciples can become over-eager in interpreting the Master's wishes. However, I wouldn't go to the other extreme and dismiss out of hand what sincere disciples say. The Master often gave messages that he expected to be shared verbally. Of course, if you hear something second-hand, it's always good to compare with the recollections of other disciples and compare it to the Master's general philosophy in his written books. But I do find disciples are generally sincere in trying to share the Master's teachings, even if their memories are not always perfect!

"Also, if you're still uncertain, it's good to feel the motive behind what people say. Are they sincerely trying to do the right thing or are they saying something to boost their ego? It's also worth bearing in mind that sometimes we can be a little selective in remembering what we want to remember. It's always convenient to think the Master would give us an exception because of our attenuating circumstances.

"Anyway, Arjun, let us not worry. The Master has quite a few wonderful characters like Tushar in his Ashram. It illustrates the Master's boundless capacity, tolerance, love and compassion that he happily accepts such a diverse range of personalities and temperaments. If we try to understand everything with our limited human mind, we may be confused. The only thing that matters is our own relationship with the Master. Just try to follow the Master's path to the best of your ability. If we look around to see what others are doing or not doing, we get caught up in their dramas and their problems. I don't know about you, but I have enough problems of my own to be dealing with!"

Arjun smiled. It all made perfect sense what Gopal was saying, but more than the words, it was the warmth, lightness of touch and balanced approach which made him understand more why the Master appreciated his dear disciple Gopal so much.

VISION AND REALITY

10,000 years ago, there was a spiritual Master who spent his formative years in an Ashram situated deep in the Himalayas. In the Ashram, the Master would spend his time absorbed in meditation, and he kept only the thinnest connection with the outer world. However, after a number of years, he felt the strongest inner command to leave the Ashram and offer spiritual wisdom to aspiring souls who were caught in their outer life. The Master's personal inclination was to stay in his blissful inner meditation but, at the same time, the Supreme showed him souls who were inwardly crying for spiritual light. The Supreme also showed the Master a vision of how this world of ignorance could be transformed into a veritable Heaven on earth.

And so, with tremendous enthusiasm to fulfil the wish of the Supreme, the Master left the Ashram and travelled without any savings or plans to a major city, where he took a simple job. On the outer plane, the Master felt lost – nothing in the Himalayas had prepared him for the hustle and bustle of city life. However, he knew the Supreme was planning and guiding everything. To his great joy, the aspiring souls he had seen in his vision started to appear in his outer life, and he was able to begin teaching the spiritual life.

However, whilst he could see the souls of his new disciples were inwardly crying for the purest spiritual life, their minds and vitals were still partly caught up in worldly attachments. The Master realised that the strictness of his former Ashram could not be transferred to city life, where individual freedom was the personal god for so many people.

Over the years, the Master attracted quite a few disciples who genuinely loved the Master. However, one day, the Master felt an inner command that the time had come to now be strict with his disciples. He felt that by being too tolerant, his disciples had become spoilt and were not making satisfactory progress. With all his compassion and love, the Master told his disciples that from now on, he wanted only those who were sincere to stay on his path: "It is not possible to enjoy the taste of sugar and salt at the same time. We have to make a choice to go forward in the spiritual life or go back to our ordinary life." The Master also strove to create a spiritual community based on the Supreme's vision of Heaven on earth.

Initially, his disciples were very enthusiastic about the Master's loftiest vision and aspiration for the highest standards. For quite a while many disciples were aspiring to live the true spiritual life, and this gave the Master tremendous joy. In these years of aspiration, the disciples were obedient to the Master's wishes. They had no time for watching TV dramas and the like, but would spend their time in selfless service or coming to the Master's varied and inspiring functions.

However, as the years went by, the Master realised that the initial burst of aspiration was becoming weaker. His disciples would attend more infrequently and were less inclined to follow all of the Master's guidance. They felt the Master did not always understand the pressures of modern life. With a heavy heart, the Master tolerated much of the disciple's new freedom. He felt that if he was too strict and unyielding, the proverbial branch would break.

There were times when the Master would inwardly commune with spiritual Masters who were in the soul's world. These spiritual Masters from Heaven would offer their love and gratitude to his divine mission on earth. But sometimes they would ask why he tolerated his disciples' disobedience and low standards. In reply, the Master on earth would say, 'It is true: my disciples' disobedience is a source of sadness. But it is very easy to forget how difficult this earthly plane is! From Heaven it is easy to hold the vision of the highest spiritual standards, but if I became strictness incarnate, will I have any disciples left? On the one hand, the Supreme has blessed me with the vision of a spiritual path that will take seekers the fastest towards their goal. But on earth, I see how hard it is to translate this vision into reality."

As the Master tolerated the disciples' freedom to some extent, some of his disciples were quite happy. Inwardly or outwardly, they said to themselves, "See, the Master allows us to do what we want. The Master always changes his mind."

The Master realised that he was caught between trying to hold on to the Supreme's lofty vision of his new spiritual path and what, in practice, he could introduce into the world. The divine in the Master was permanently in touch with God's highest Bliss and Ecstasy, but the human in the Master was discouraged by earth's ingratitude and lack of receptivity. This time his yogi-friends from the soul's word reminded him: is not every spiritual Master misunderstood? Is there any spiritual Master who did not come 2,000 years too early for earth's receptivity? The Master felt the need to talk to his disciples.

"My dear children, this spiritual path is not created by me. It is created by the Supreme himself. If we want to realise God, we have to do it in God's Way. You may think your way is better, but if we want to deliver a letter to the Pope, we have to travel to Rome, no matter how difficult or inconvenient it may seem to be. We may feel it is much faster to get on Concorde and fly to New York in two hours. We may like the speed of Concorde and feel we are travelling very fast, but if we fly to New York we will never be able to have a meeting with the Pope. To some extent, you can do what you want. But if you want to realise God, you have to do it in God's own Way, never your own way.

"Sometimes, I have set guidelines in the spiritual life that are 100% for your own spiritual benefit, but later I realised that people are not ready to accept, and if I did not relax my standards to some extent, there would be an inner rebellion. Whilst I can tolerate different standards as a matter of necessity, it does not mean that this is what I want. There is a big difference between my tolerance and my approval. It is very important to bear in mind that just because you see other people following a slower path, it does not mean that is something to which you should aspire. If you want to win the race, you have to run at the speed of the lead runner – not stay at the back of the pack, chatting to people who have no interest in finishing the race, to say nothing of winning.

"In my early days, how many hours I would spend in meditation. My life was austerity incarnate. I feel that this path I am offering is considerably easier than the one I took. The Supreme, out of His infinite Bounty, has offered a new spiritual path for this modern, restless civilisation. I am not asking you to follow the austerity of the ancient years – those days are over. However, the problem is that when the Supreme offers an easier path, it is not enough, and we always want something even easier than the easiest. As I have said many times, God-realisation is not like drinking instant coffee. Outer wealth, outer convenience and scientific achievement – I have nothing against these – but they do not take you even one inch closer to your goal. Our path is the path of the heart; the path of the psychic being. If we want to please the Supreme, we have to feel His Way is the right way. Our shortcuts not only do not take us any closer, but in fact push us further away.

"My dear children, it is up to you. It is your choice how quickly you want to proceed in the spiritual life. But I do hope that at least some will value my vision of the spiritual life – which is none other than the Vision of the Supreme. If even one disciple of mine can realise God, I will be unimaginably happy, plus divinely proud. So, let us see how far we can go to reach the Supreme's Vision of Heaven on earth."

ILLUMINATION ON DUALITY

Prisha was a devoted disciple of Swami Adeshananda. However her husband Chandan had no real interest in spirituality. When Prisha went to see her Guru, Chandan would work in his garden.

However, on one occasion, curiosity got the better of Chandan and he joined his wife when the Swami visited the house of a local disciple. During this meeting, Swami Adeshananda gave an informal talk on the underlying oneness of creation. He said that when we enter the highest meditation, we go beyond duality – beyond good and evil ¬– and see God in everything. Prisha and the other disciples were inspired with the knowledge that, ultimately, we would be able to see, feel and understand God was ever-present – omniscient and omnipresent. However, Chandan inwardly scoffed at this philosophy of 'beyond right and wrong'. He said to himself, "This is a wonderful philosophy. No right and wrong! Well, let me try this new philosophy!"

Later that day, Chandan took half of his wife's savings and gambled the money on a horse. The horse didn't win, and when Prisha found out half her savings had been squandered she felt miserable. Distraught, she said, "Chandan, where did my savings go?"

Chandan replied, "It's OK Prisha. As your Guru said, 'God is in everything.' God is in the bookmaker and so I placed a bet. True, I lost the money, but we have to go beyond the duality of winning and losing. God is in both winning and losing bets."

Prisha was upset. She was upset to lose half of her savings that she hoped to give as a love-offering to her Master, but she was more upset that her husband seemed to be deliberately misinterpreting her Master's teachings.

She related this sorry tale to her Master. After hearing her story, Swami Adeshananda replied, "I understand your frustration and disappointment, but do not be overly upset. Let us try to be detached. Your heart's offering and sincerity I value infinitely more than the amount of money you give me. In this case, you have done nothing wrong, so let us try to give the experience to God, who, ultimately, will be able to transform our suffering into joy.

"However," and a broad smile appeared on the face of Swami Adeshananda, "at the same time, God is inspiring me to teach your husband a lesson. Prisha, your husband is very fond of apple pies, no?"

"Yes, Master" said Prisha.

"Very good. I would like you to bake your husband a beautiful pie. But instead of apples, I would like you to substitute cow dung."

"Cow dung, Master? Are you serious?"

"Yes," said the Master, "trust me." With a small grin, the Master said, "Let us see whether or not your husband can still see God in everything!"

A few days later, Prisha baked the cake with cow dung and invited the Master back to her house.

At the request of her Master, she served a piece of cow dung pie to both her Master and her husband. Her husband greedily took a bite out of the pie, but soon spat it out.

"What is happening?!" exclaimed Chandan. "This tastes terrible."

Swami Adeshananda then took a big bite out of the pie and said, "To me, this pie tastes of the sweetest nectar. Truly I feel God's sweetness and goodness in this pie – even though it is made of cow dung." To prove his point, the Master took another big bite and appeared to relish the food.

"I am not trying to make fun of you Chandan, but it is a mistake to misinterpret God's loftiest Philosophy. From the highest philosophical and spiritual viewpoint, God is in everything. But we have to know whether or not we have the spiritual realisation to actually see and feel this. God is in dirty water and God is in clean water. But God is also in wisdom. So, what shall we drink? You can say God is more manifest in the pure water.

"In my case, during my highest meditation, I have gone beyond the world of duality. For me, the Immanence of God in this world is not mere philosophy, but a living reality. That is why I can eat cow dung and feel God's Nectar.

"At the moment, my disciples don't have this realisation – which is why we have to use our wisdom in following actions that bring us closer to God. When you have realised God, you can go to a bookmaker's and be unaffected. But until you have realised the highest, the forces of worldly ignorance will just take you further away from the goal."

Chandan slinked away. He never went to see his wife's Guru again, but at the same time, he never again made fun of his philosophy!

SPEAKING UP

Many thousands of years ago, there was an Indian spiritual Master who had many devoted disciples. The Master felt the most effective form of teaching was silence. He told his disciples that to really understand his philosophy and teachings it was necessary to silence the mind and listen to the still, inner voice within. However, the Master also found that, out of necessity, he needed to give specific teachings on aspects of his spiritual path.

As books were very rare and expensive, this Master did not write any of his teachings down, but relied on speaking informally to disciples. Sometimes his teachings and talks were slightly misinterpreted; two disciples could come out of the same talk and remember very different things! But, fortunately, this Master lived a very long time, and when he felt he was not being understood, he would repeat his philosophy and teachings until they were widely known.

Despite living for a long-time, the Master eventually left the body, and his disciples dearly missed the outer presence of their Master. However, by and large they continued following the Master's way of life, and the Ashram continued in a similar vein to when the Master's physical presence was outwardly guiding it.

After several years, Hari was very happy to see the Master's spiritual path still thriving and the essence of his teachings still being maintained. Every now and then he could see his fellow disciples following their own ideas, and doing things a little differently from how his Master had done them. Often, he felt that these were not such serious changes, and disciples needed the freedom to follow the path to the best of their understanding. And, more importantly, he had plenty of his own problems to try and solve!

However, although he wished to avoid any discussion, he sometimes saw things which left him inwardly concerned, and he started questioning whether or not he had remembered his Master's teaching correctly.

On one occasion, he went along to a talk about his Master's philosophy and was surprised to find that other members of the Ashram had started to charge members of the public for attending the lecture. When Hari heard this, all his joy and enthusiasm drained away, and it left him feeling inwardly perturbed. He knew the Ashram was short of money, but at the same time, he felt his Master had really been very clear that on his path he wished to offer spirituality free – to avoid any commercial charges. His Master taught that spirituality was everyone's birthright, and lectures given in his name should be available for free.

Hari was quite torn – his natural instinct was to say nothing and keep a low profile, but he was equally uncomfortable with allowing the situation to continue. After a few days, there was a meeting in the Ashram and everyone seemed quite happy, though Hari was still very much thinking about this change in philosophy. As the meeting progressed, Hari realised that nobody was going to say anything about charging the public for lectures. So, with great reluctance, he stepped forward and said he felt this was against the Master's wishes. It was not the most elegant speech. It was blunt and to the point and he felt quite self-conscious. There was a degree of murmuring, but another senior disciple then spoke up and agreed that this was not what the Master intended.

The older disciple continued that although finances could be better, it is important that we don't undermine the Master's wishes because of temporary expediency. The Master himself had never worried about money, but had always sought to follow God's Will, and trust that the necessary money would arrive just in time – as it frequently did.

After this inspiring speech, it was agreed that in the future the Ashram would always offer meditations and public lectures for free – just as the Master intended.

Hari felt much better for speaking up and was relieved to have overcome his hesitancy to make a fuss. The interesting thing is that over the next few days many other disciples came up to Hari and said they were very grateful he had spoken up about this issue. They too had felt quite uneasy about it, but were not so confident to raise it. It was definitely different now the Master was not in the body, but Hari realised that sometimes it really was the right thing to speak up – even if personally he would much prefer to keep a quiet life.

TABLE OF CONTENTS

Abhik's passing	11
Devotion	17
What's up?	26
Maintaining standards	31
Appreciation	41
'Guru said', part 1	48
'Guru said', part 2	55
Beyond likes and dislikes	63
At the restaurant	71
Musical arrangements	78
The mind's rigidity	91
Is the fruit really blue?	99
Unconditional forgiveness	104
Detachment inner and outer	111
The Secret teaching	121
An awkward character	128
Getting new disciples	135
The Model Ashram	146
Chat Groups	155
Favourite aspect of the Master	167
The Aura of the Master	174
Accepting disciples in their own way	182
The Smoking Disciple	185
Vision and Reality	191
Illumination on duality	196
Speaking up	200

About the Author

Tejvan Pettinger was born 1976 in Runnymeade, Great Britain. He grew up in Yorkshire. From 1995-99 he studied PPE at Lady Margaret Hall, Oxford University.

In 1999, he became a disciple of the spiritual Master, Sri Chinmoy. He is a member of the Oxford Sri Chinmoy Centre where he offers meditation classes.

Tejvan Pettinger's previous books include:

- *Happiness Will Follow You* (2010) Ganapati Press.
- *Walking Along the Sunlit Path - Tejvan's Stories* (2011) The Goldenshore.
- *Cracking Economics* (2017) Octopus Press.
- *What Would Keynes do?* (2018) Octopus Press.
- *Stories from the Spiritual Life, part 1,* (2018) Ganapati Press.
- *Economics Without the Boring Bits* (2021) Wellbeck.

Tejvan is an amateur cyclist and competes for Sri Chinmoy Cycling Team. His results include:

- UK National Hill Climb Championship - 1st (2013)

Vilas Silverton - Artist

Vilas is a visionary artist, who lives in Bristol. He is also a student of Sri Chinmoy, who has completed several long-distance cycling challenges, including the Indian Pacific Wheel Race across Australia.

www.ingramcontent.com/pod-product-compliance
Lightning Source LLC
Chambersburg PA
CBHW020854090426
42736CB00008B/364